The CATFISH BOOK

The CATfISH BOOK

LINDA CRAWFORD

A Muscadine Book

University Press of Mississippi

JACKSON AND LONDON

94 93 92 91   4 3 2 1

The paper in this book meets the guidelines for perma-
nence and durability of the Committee on Production
Guidelines for Book Longevity of the Council on Library Resources.

Designed by Robin Evans Smith

Library of Congress Cataloging-in-Publication Data

Crawford, Linda, 1953–
    The catfish book / by Linda Crawford.
      p. cm.
    "A Muscadine book."
    Includes bibliographical references and index.
    ISBN 0-87805-502-9
    1. Catfishes. 2. Catfishes—Folklore.
  3. Cookery (Catfish) I. Title.
QL637.9.S5C73 1991
597'.52—dc20   90-28686
                            CIP

British Library Cataloging-in-Publication data available

CONTENTS

FOREWORD

ALMOST all the Southerners I know have a deeply felt association with catfish. It is the most "southern" of fish and figures largely in the diet of their youth. It did in mine, in any event, and was undoubtedly the first fish I ever had the good fortune to sample.

To this day, if I see catfish on a menu (and it is being seen with increasing frequency on some of the most sophisticated menus of the nation), I feel a compulsion to order it. And if I ever travel South, it is one of the foods (along with barbecue) I feel absolutely compelled to order to satisfy my cravings. And when I do order it south of the Mason and Dixon, I want it well coated with cornmeal, fried until crisp outside, and served piping hot.

I have often recalled with fond memories the outings my family made in my early years with neighbors and friends to Four Mile Lake, a watering place near my small hometown in Mississippi. Gliding about on the water were small pleasure craft, fishlines dangling from the sides, ready to haul in the catfish.

Whenever a sufficient bath of catfish had been hauled aboard, they would be carried ashore and cleaned with hunting knives. There were inevitably hot vats of oil sitting on the shore and picnic tables not far away. The fish would be dredged in a large bucket of cornmeal and cooked in the hot fat until crisp and succulent and moist within. The fish would be eaten with bottled ketchup, a little Worcestershire sauce, a little Tabasco, and lemon wedges. And sweetened iced tea.

Within the past few years, as the market for catfish has expanded and they have become more widely available throughout the nation, I have noticed scores of ways in which they have been cooked and presented—Florentine (with spinach), Veronique (with grapes), au vin blanc (in a white wine sauce), amandine (with almonds), and so on. Catfish are, in truth, one of the most versatile of all fish for cooking. They are tender in texture, delicate in flavor, and respond well to most known food preparations—sauteeing, frying, baking, soup-making, and so on.

The Catfish Book is one of the finest, most definitive books on catfish cookery I've ever encountered. It embraces all aspects of the fish including its history, the manifold qualities of the fish, and recipes. It should be an essential addition to anyone who pretends to have a complete library of fish cookery.

Craig Claiborne
East Hampton, N.Y.

ACKNOWLEDGMENTS

WRITING a first book is a very scary, yet exhilarating experience. I want to thank my editor and friend, JoAnne Prichard, and everyone else at University Press of Mississippi for giving me the opportunity. Their ever-constant encouragement and patience provided the impetus I needed to undertake and finally to complete this project.

My editor's husband, the irrepressible Willie Morris, generously gave suggestions and ultimately a jacket quote. His much-needed words of praise eased my doubts and enabled me to continue writing.

The staff at the South Delta Library Services in Rolling Fork and Yazoo City, Mississippi, were always supportive in helping me to locate research materials. I especially need to thank John Ellzey who allowed me to load the inter-library loan service with research requests, and Susie Bull, who helped to proofread the final manuscript. The entire staff kept abreast of my progress, always seeming to sense when I required encouragement and then dispensing it as needed.

The Catfish Institute and the Catfish Farmers of America were generous with information about the industry, and I thank them for their invaluable assistance. My special gratitude also goes to the Simmons Catfish Farms of Yazoo City, Mississippi, who were patient and helpful with my last minute verifications of processing procedures.

Finally, I want to acknowledge my gratitude to my grandmother, Belle Crawford, for giving me an appreciation of the South's favorite fish, and to my family for giving me the courage to write about it.

WHEN I was a youngster, my favorite and most frequent fishing companion was my grandmother, perhaps because she recognized in me the same obsessive enjoyment of the sport. You had to be a bit obsessive to do it the way we did.

The top of the Texas panhandle, where I grew up and where my grandmother lived, cannot be identified as a fisherman's paradise. There were no tree-lined lakes or mighty rivers to float along. Instead we frequented the shadeless man-made ponds and tanks that had been built to water cattle and horses. Most of the ponds had catfish in them because it would have been wasteful not to. Why have a pond if you don't have catfish? You might as well leave out the water.

My grandmother lived in Spearman, a big town of over 3,000 people in comparison to Gruver, where I lived. She would call, all excited about each new fishing hole she had discovered. By the time I got there, she would have a picnic basket packed with Spam and bread, and the fishing tackle would be sitting by the back steps. We would load everything into her car and drive out to spend hours in the relentless sun and incessant winds of the Texas panhandle. We loved it.

It was Grandma who taught me the fundamental secret of successful fishing—keep the hook in the water.

"Too many people can't keep their hook in the water," she'd tell me. "You can't catch anything by looking at your bait."

I was grown before I realized that advice applied to more than catching fish.

It was also she who taught me the "right" way to "skin a cat," and that the only way to cook one was to roll it in cornmeal and fry it in a big black skillet.

Some high-minded fishing manuals condemn catfishing as an activity unequal to the pursuit of other fish. But although I have caught bass, trout, crappie, perch, and numerous others, none of these experiences can match the enjoyment I got from those times with my grandma.

Maybe that is part of the appeal that catfish hold for southerners. Of all the game fish available throughout the region, cats are perhaps the most common and the most universally sought by children and adults, singly and in groups—not just for sport or for eating, but for the generation and recreation of memories.

My grandmother is dead now, but I think of her often—and she always has a fishing pole in one hand and a squirming catfish in the other. I sure hope they have catfish in heaven, or Grandma's bound to be disappointed.

The
CAT*f*ISH
BOOK

CATS AND CATTING

OF all the fishes in the South, none is more often associated with the region than catfish. Southerners since the prehistoric Indians have gone "catting," as fishing for catfish is sometimes called, and have caught and eaten almost every variety of the native catfishes.

Elvas, one of the chroniclers of the DeSoto expedition in the sixteenth century, gave one of the earliest historical reports of catfish when he described the fish caught in the Mississippi River and its tributaries: "There was a fish called 'bagre,' a third of which was head; and it had large spines like a sharp shoemaker's awl at either side of its throat and along the sides. . . .

In the river, there were some of one hundred and one hundred and fifty pounds. Many of them were caught with the hook."

Thomas Jefferson in his *Notes on the State of Virginia* also made special mention of "catfishes" weighing over 100 pounds in the Mississippi River.

Anyone describing catfish is likely to mention that they form an especially ugly group, but as *The Compleat Angler* reported of seventeenth century English bullheads, they taste better than they look.

Cotton Mather, that Puritan icon of sobriety, wrote disapprovingly of fishing in 1721, "Alas, the Ministers of the Gospel now fish, not with Nets, but with Rods; and after long angling, and baiting, and waiting, how few are caught!"

In time, "sport" fishing came to be seen as a predominantly upperclass male activity for catching "game" fish, such as trout or bass. The equipment is more expensive and the pursuit more time consuming, and therefore less efficient for food procurement.

It is said that the status of a fish can be determined by the expense and complexity of the equipment needed to catch it. That being the case, catfish are seen as a "rough" fish, suitable for slaves and the poor, because they can be legally caught with seines and with trotlines. "Gamer" species, such as bass and trout, face a more sporting end.

Catfish can be and are caught by people of both sexes and of all ages and socio-economic groups, both because the fish are widespread geographically and because they can be landed by a variety of methods. Catfish are often caught with bamboo or cane poles, but a simple baited line from an overhanging limb will do just as well.

Glenn Morris clearly outlined this "corrolation between the economic and social stature of fishermen, the game they pursue, and the method they prefer to use," in his article on "Fishing" in the *Encyclopedia of Southern Culture*. "At the bottom of the economic scale, the preferred fishing is catfish/bream by cork or bobber fishing/bait casting, bass/spinner fishing is the choice of blue collar families, bass fly-rod fishing of white collar workers, and artificial fly fishing for native trout is the preserve of upper income professionals."

Signs proclaiming that store owners have "gone fishing" produce images of lazy days devoid of strenuous or productive activity. For, as an 1897 sign declared, "To-day, I am fishing for cats, and when I go a catin', I go a catin'."

A cane pole with a float and a hook on its line is a veritable symbol of long hours of a fisherman sleepily waiting for a bite. As Mississippi Supreme Court Justice James Robertson stated in his 1990 opinion in *Dycus v. Sillers*, "Many think fishing the most leisurely of leisure activities, the positive pursuit of the lazy." Willie Morris reminisced in *North Toward Home*, "We did cane-pole fishing, both to save money and because it was lazier. . . ."

This is one reason why pole fishing was forbidden to slaves, for no slave owner enjoyed seeing them "loaf," even when the inactivity produced a positive, and edible, result.

Catfishing was seen as suitable for slaves when the fish were caught in nets, a more strenuous method than pole fishing, or on trotlines, which allows the fisherman to absent himself from the activity. Catfish are so widespread that at least one species can be found in virtually every body of water in the South, and a large channel cat, flathead, or blue catfish could feed an entire family easily. On the Davis plantation in antebellum Alabama, large cats weighing over thirty pounds were caught daily, and in the Mississippi tributaries, they could be much larger.

In *Life on the Mississippi* Mark Twain wrote that during Joliet and Marquette's 1673 exploration of the Mississippi River, "a big catfish collided with Marquette's canoe and startled him; and reasonably enough, for he had been warned by the Indians that he was on a foolhardy journey, and even a fatal one, for the river contained a demon whose roar could be heard at great distance and who would engulf them in the abyss where he dwelled." Twain continued: "I have seen a Mississippi catfish that was more than six feet long and weighed 250 pounds; and if Marquette's fish was the fellow to that one, he had a fair right to think the river's roaring demon was come."

Catfish are still often seen as a "soul" food, and a section of town with predominantly black residents may be labeled "catfish row." This term was popularized in the George Gershwin musical *Porgy and Bess,* which is set on Catfish Row in Charleston, South Carolina. Vicksburg, Mississippi's Catfish Row is familiar to many Southerners who know it from David Cohn's often quoted comment that "the Mississippi Delta begins in the lobby of the Peabody Hotel in Memphis and ends on Catfish Row in Vicksburg."

Freed slaves sold catfish to both white and black customers. Wash Rose of Yazoo County, Mississippi, earned much of the money he needed to set up his blacksmith shop and real estate ventures after the Civil War by selling catfish; and in turn-of-the-century Yazoo City phonebooks, many blacks listed their occupation as fishseller.

Cats have also been associated with poor whites and the riverboat people, who virtually lived off catfish and sold them at the ports.

The status of catfish is probably also affected by the fact that cats are among the most popular gamefish of southern women and children, two groups generally excluded from the corps of "serious fishermen." Contrary to public opinion, many women do enjoy fishing at every opportunity, or as Estella in Ellen Douglas's *Black Cloud, White Cloud* asserted, "Baby or no baby, I got to go fishing after such a fine rain."

Women do bait their own hooks, remove the catch, clean, and, of course, cook it, too. Douglas's Estella was an accom-

plished fisherman, as attested by Miss Anna's instructions to her
son, "Steve, watch Estella, so you'll know how to do it right."

The nicknames of catfish provide further indications of their
lowly image. A person referred to as a bullhead, chucklehead,
mudcat, squealer, or flathead would be justifiably insulted. It is
possible to like catfish, and to enjoy eating them, without want-
ing to resemble one.

Despite the negative imagery, catfish continue to occupy a
special place in southern lore. It is, as Justice Robertson stated,
"The ubiquitous catfish, of the family Ictaluridae, the blue, the
channel and the flathead, of whom legends transcend the fact-
fiction dichotomy."

Prevention magazine reported in June 1988 that researchers at
the University of California had analyzed catfish slime and discovered a number of possibly beneficial uses, including "a co-
agulant that helps close injured blood vessels; antibiotics, anti-
inflammatory agents and a chemical that directs production of a
glue-like material that aids healing." They did not recommend
direct application, however, for reasons anyone having been spined
by a catfish can surmise. It is just one more of those "fact-fiction"
dichotomies that the slime which might someday be used to heal,
burns like wildfire, causing the punctures to become infected.

Catfish, especially the modern farm-raised channel cats, are of
great dietary benefit too, being low in fat and calories, while high
in protein. This benefit is counteracted by the southern penchant

for deep-frying huge quantities of the fish and serving it with mounds of french fries, hushpuppies, and coleslaw.

The southern viewpoint seems to be, "I don't care if it is good for you; I like it anyway."

Ugly or healthy, trash or game, catfish holds a special place in southern life and lore.

MEETING THE CATFISH FAMILY

SOUTHERNERS have a special affection for their native catfish, but to fully appreciate this particularly ugly, flat-headed, broad-mouthed, bewhiskered fish, one should understand its place in the grand scheme of things and look at some of the other cats in its family tree.

Southern catfish are a diverse group and, like any respectable southern family, have some rather eccentric relatives. There are over 2,000 species of catfish worldwide, in about thirty different families in the suborder Ostariophysi. The smallest, such as the skunk catfish and the pygmy corydoras, measure less than 1 ½ inches long and are often kept in home aquariums. The largest are the Eurasian catfish, also known as sheatfish or wels, which can grow up to fifteen feet long and weigh over 600 pounds.

In general, catfish have two to four pairs of long whisker-like barbels, broad mouths, strong spines on their pectoral and dorsal fins, and no scales. They have existed at least since the Eocene period, some 60 million years ago. Most catfish have a thick, rubbery skin. Others, of the Doradidae (corydoras), Callichthyide and Loricariidae (sucker catfish) groups, are "armor-plated."

There are several unusual types represented in the catfish family. The giant Eurasian sheatfish (*Silurus glanis*), known as wels, are peculiar looking even for catfish. They have very small dorsal fins and very long anal fins almost merging with their caudal fins, giving them elongated bodies much like eels. Although a 750-pound wels was once reported in czarist Russia, 200-pound specimens are now considered large. The *Wallogonia attu* of Indonesia, one of the biggest wels, hunts its prey from just below the surface, leaping out of the water to make its catch. Fish are their main food, but these cats are said to eat anything and everything that ventures into their territories, including birds and small mammals swimming on the surface. There is even a story about a child being devoured by one of the voracious giants. More often the fish are caught for human consumption.

If you are looking for a skeleton in the catfish family closet, start with the glass catfish (*Kryptopterus bicirrhis*), a native of India and Indonesia. A popular resident of home aquariums, its body organs are enclosed in a sac which is compressed right behind the head. The body of the fish is beautifully translucent and its skeleton fully visible. This fish's tranquility as well as its transparency causes it to be easily overlooked in a crowd, but like many a timid relative, closer inspection reveals a serene inner beauty.

The electric catfish (*Malapterus electricus*) is the shocker in the group. Weighing up to fifty pounds, this African native stuns its prey with an electrical current of up to 800 volts. The ancient Egyptians considered it sacred but sometimes ate it anyway, forever dispelling any advantage of divinity.

The nonconformist is the 3 ¼ inch upside-down catfish (*Synodontis nigriventris*) of central West Africa. It begins its life conventionally enough, but as it grows older, everything, even its coloring, becomes topsy-turvy as it faces the world from a different angle. There are about 150 species of this unusual fish, which is believed to adopt this perverse attitude in order to eat algae from the underside of leaves that have fallen into the streams it inhabits.

One of the most unkempt relatives is the bushy-mouth catfish (*Xenocara dolichoptera*) of South America. It has a large growth of whiskers covering the front of its head in addition to the barbels found on other catfish.

As in some families, there is also a member who might easily be described as a "worm." Africa's eel catfish (*Channallabes apus*) looks like a foot-long worm with whiskers.

Although the eel catfish may look like a snake, it is not blood-thirsty. That description better fits the parasitic catfish (*Trichomycteridae*) of South America. These tiny fish, known as candiru, swim into the gills of larger fish and feed on their blood. Like the relative rudely intruding wherever he isn't welcome, this fish has been known to invade the most private orifices of unpleasantly surprised swimmers and is removed only with difficulty and pain.

The religious member of the family is described in *The Wise Encyclopedia of Cooking:* "A certain catfish of the genius *arius* is called Easter of Holy Cross fish because the shape of its skull and back show a distinct resemblance to Christ on the cross. Each side of the body bears a faint figure of a kneeling person. These fish are edible and delicious and run in exceptionally large schools during the Lenten season along the shores of South and Central America. Devoutly religious people abstain from eating them before Easter."

The rover of the family is an import from tropical Asia which has escaped into Florida rivers. The walking catfish (*Clarias batrachus*), also known as the Pla duk dam or the albino clarias, grows up to eighteen inches long. This determined wanderer can move overland to another body of water by pushing itself along the ground with its tail and lifting its head with its strong front fins. The walking catfish is able to live up to twelve hours out of water because it has a huge lung-like breathing organ opening off the gills which enables it to breathe air. It is also one of the few species which naturally exists as albinos.

Excluding this nomadic import, there are approximately two dozen species of catfish in the United States, with over half of them native to the South. All North American catfish are of the family Ictaluridae.

The smallest of these are the madtoms, whose name is derived from "mad tomcat," and is pronounced accordingly. Madtoms grow to only two to five inches long, depending on the variety. One identifyng characteristic is a poison gland in the spine, which discourages predators, waders, and shell-seekers.

There are about half a dozen kinds of madtoms found in the southern streams, creeks, and low gradient lakes. They are named descriptively with such monikers as "least" madtom, "brindled" madtom, "speckled" and "freckled" madtoms. The longfin madtom has the interesting scientific name of *"Noturus funebris,"* roughly meaning "funeral madtom" because of its dark, somber coloration.

There are several species of bullhead catfish, so named because of their big heads. It might have been the bullhead that was the subject of the James Kirk Paulding story first published in the *Daily Louisville Advertiser* October 17, 1831: "I was chuckle head enough to go down the Mississippi fishing for lawyers one day. . . .

I call catfish lawyers—'case you see they're all head and [their] head all mouth."

Bullheads are locally known as "mudcats" because of their affinity for the muddy bottoms of lakes and rivers. It is said that one of the primary survival skills of the bullhead is its ability to live in waters too muddy for other fish. This adaptability is enhanced by the catfish's barbels, which act as sensory organs in its quest for food among the muck.

The palatability of these fish is either "muddy" or "the best eating," depending on the individual. Bullheads are scavengers eating a wide variety of foods, so that their flavor is largely determined by their recent diet.

The brown bullhead (*Ictalurus nebulosus*) is the most common. Also called the horned pout or the speckled bullhead, the brown

BROWN BULLHEAD

bullhead grows to about eighteen inches long and to a weight of about four pounds. Their color is not the solid brown that the name might indicate. On top they are a dark yellowish brown that grows lighter toward the belly, which is yellow or milk-white. The tail is very slightly concave. The flesh, like that of all bullheads, is red or pink. The nickname "horned pout" comes from the hornlike growths near their mouths.

In the spring these catfish scrape hollows in the mud or sand in shallow areas to make their nests, each of which holds from 2,000 to 6,000 eggs. The male stands guard over the eggs until they hatch. Then both parents defend their young until the fry reach about one inch long. The young bullheads tend to travel in schools, which makes them easy prey for fishermen.

The black bullhead (*Ictalurus melas*) is smaller than the brown, usually reaching about twelve inches long and just under three

BLACK BULLHEAD

pounds, and is very widespread, being especially tolerant of murky waters. Their color is dark olive to black on the top and cream to yellow on the bottom (it may become more golden during breeding). The fins are usually darker than the body, and the tail is slightly rounded at the corners.

The yellow bullhead (*Ictalurus natalis*) is usually dark yellow with darker blotches and a yellow or white stomach. The fins are

YELLOW BULLHEAD

the same color as the body and the tail is squared or slightly rounded. This catfish makes its nests in water from eighteen inches to several feet deep, and like the other bullheads, it guards its young for several weeks after hatching has occurred. Adults tend to be from twelve to eighteen inches long and weigh about three pounds. Some fishermen think the yellow is the best tasting of the bullheads, asserting that its flavor is that of a "real catfish."

The flat bullhead (*Ictalurus platycephalus*), which grows to about two pounds and fifteen inches, is a mottled olive to yellowish

brown, with a dark area across the base of its dorsal fin. All fins but the pectoral are edged in black. The tail tends to be

FLAT BULLHEAD

slightly concave. As its name suggests, its most prominent characteristic is a flattened head.

The white catfish (*Ictalurus catus*) is pale blue on top and silvery below. Its moderately forked tail sometimes causes it to be

mistaken for the channel cat, although it is smaller and has no spots. The white cat reaches a length of about two feet and a

WHITE CATFISH

weight of about three to five pounds.

The spotted bullhead (*Ictalurus serracanthus*) resembles the white catfish but has small yellowish spots on its sides.

The channel cat (*Ictalurus punctatus*) is most preferred by fisherman epicures and is the species most often raised on catfish

farms. Important as both a commercial and game fish, the channel cat, which can weigh well over twenty pounds, is

CHANNEL CATFISH

widely distributed in streams and lakes throughout the South.

Also known as prairie trout, fiddler, chucklehead, fork-tail cat, speckled catfish, lady cat, silver cat, willow cat, whiskered walleye, and squealer, the channel cat is a trim fish with a deeply forked tail and is silvery olive or slate-blue on top with a silvery white belly. Younger fish have dark spots or speckles along the sides, but these disappear with age.

During breeding season, channel cats tend to become darker. Eggs are laid in a gelatinous mass and are guarded by the male for the six-to-ten-day incubation. As with the other catfish, the young fry travel in schools for a time, but then separate to feed singly as they grow older.

A channel cat is indiscriminately omnivorous and eats all kinds of things, animal and plant, dead or alive, found in its environment. It feeds in the channels at dusk and moves into the shallows at night. It prefers swifter, cleaner water than the bullheads and enjoys a reputation as a "good fighter." A fifty-eight pound channel cat was reported caught in South Carolina, but five-to-ten pound adults are more common.

One of the ugliest southern catfish is also one of the biggest. The flathead catfish (*Pylodictis olivaris*) has the same broad, whis-

FLATHEAD OR YELLOW CATFISH

kered head as the other catfish, except that it looks as if something heavy has been dropped on it, repeatedly, right between the eyes. Its appearance is not improved by its protruding lower jaw.

The nicknames attached to this square-tailed fish are the "yellow cat," because of its yellowish-brown coloring and the "appallosa" because younger fish are slightly mottled; but pigmentation tends to become irrelevant with a head that ugly.

What the flathead lacks in beauty, it attains in size, with individuals weighing over 100 pounds being caught in southern rivers. The International Game Fish Association's rod-and-reel record for a flathead is ninety-eight pounds, but much larger yellow cats have been snared on trotlines. A 150-pound flathead was reported caught near the mouth of the Big Black River in Mississippi in 1954, and others over 100 pounds have been taken in recent years.

Flatheads are said to scavenge less than other catfish and to prefer live food. An eighteen-pound flathead caught in Lake Travis, Texas, reportedly was found to have an unplucked chicken in its belly. A flathead that was eating ducklings in a Washington pond was dubbed the "monster of the black lagoon" in the April 22, 1989, issue of the *Houston Post*. The giants are loners, lurking in deep "catholes" during the day and waiting until twilight to prowl the shallows for their prey. Some of the flatheads caught on trotlines had swallowed whole smaller fish that took the bait.

Despite such competition, the king of the southern catfish is the blue cat (*Ictalurus furcatus*). It is a much more attractive fish than the flathead, being bluish-silver or grey, with deeply forked

BLUE CATFISH

tail, a slightly protruding upper jaw, and a more moderately flattened head. This species, which frequents swifter, clearer waters than other catfish, makes its nests in the shelter of a submerged rock or log. Both parents guard the nest and the young.

Heavy salt-water tackle is used to catch these huge fish, which can weigh well over 100 pounds. Also called the "fulton," the "blue fulton," the "humpback," or simply "Mississippi catfish," this is probably the titan, "big as a man," that got away from Mark Twain's Huckleberry Finn and Jim. It was also the subject of antebellum tales of giants weighing over 200 pounds, big enough to capsize riverboats.

In one tall tale, a tethered hog fell overboard and was swallowed by a great blue cat. The riverboat captain had to shoot the fish as it dragged the vessel, laden with passengers and baggage, upriver.

A blue cat weighing 150 pounds given to the Smithsonian Natural Science Museum in 1879 is the heaviest verifiable catch. More recently, a 130-pounder was taken from a Tennessee reservoir in 1976.

These giants have the added attraction of having a tasty, white flesh, which is fortunate considering how much of them there is to eat.

GOING A-CATTING

THE catfish's usefulness as a source of insult is not limited to its appearance or its lifestyle. A particularly unkind person is as "mean as a catfish," and someone who is very loud and obnoxious might be referred to as "a real catfish."

These unflattering comments about the catfish's personality are earned in part by its understandable aversion to being unpleasantly stuck on a hook. Finding itself pulled toward shore, the average catfish will pull back—hard. This feistiness has earned the catfish a well-deserved reputation as a "sport" fish, the assumption being that the more difficult something is to achieve the more "sporting" it is. Catfish oblige by making the whole process as difficult as possible.

Despite all difficulties, or perhaps because of them, southerners have long enjoyed the perennial battle between man and cat.
Legends abound of giant catfish swimming in southern rivers
and of treacherous, deep "catholes" where the monsters mali-
ciously wait to drag some incautious victim underwater. Mark
Twain told of Huckleberry Finn and Jim using a rabbit as bait
to "catch a catfish that was as big as a man, being six foot
two inches long, and weighed over two hundred pounds. We
couldn't handle him, of course; he would 'a' flung us into Illinois."

References to "catting," as fishing for catfish is sometimes
called, are common in both historical and legendary accounts. In
several of these, other fish caught are thrown back, as described in
a 1865 *Spirit of Times & Sportsman:* "When we go a catting, we
goes a catting, and throws trout back into the water to pay 'em
for their imperdence of biting."

Methods of catching catfish vary. The most common continues
to be a cane pole, sinker, and some type of live bait. Minnows,
crickets, worms, grasshoppers, chicken livers or gizzards, calf's
liver, crayfish, shrimp, whole or cut perch, shad, or other fish
have been used, in addition to Huckleberry's rabbit and the
whole, unplucked chicken reportedly found in the belly of that
eighteen-pound flathead catfish caught in Lake Travis, Texas. A
tall tale by A. D. Livingston, recounted in *Field and Stream* in
April 1990, insists that skinned billy goats are the best bait
for catching big catfish. There are also adherents for the use of

coagulated beef blood, corn, doughballs, cheese, Ivory soap, and a wide variety of "stink baits" and artificial lures. A variety of commercial and homemade concoctions are available that will make even the artificial lures stink, the assumption being that because catfish are natural scavengers they prefer things that smell. "Dip baits" are short, concentrically grooved plastic worms that are anointed with a smelly mess, often with a high butterfat cheese base to which substances such as turtle guts or beef blood have been added. A few fishermen take the added precaution of borrowing from the European tradition of spitting on the bait before throwing it into the water. Others handle the bait as little as possible so that the human scent will not be detected.

Interestingly enough, catfish can find food even after their olfactory organs have been removed, according to a 1967 article in *Science* magazine. An estimated 100,000 taste buds cover virtually the entire skin surface of catfish but are especially dense on their barbels, enabling catfish to detect food in still water from more than eighteen and one-half feet away.

Although the practice is illegal in many states, some fisher-men resort to "chumming" or "baiting the hole" by throwing dead minnows, corn, water-soaked grain, or other bits of bait into the area being fished to encourage the fish to feed indis-criminately. When the procedure is accomplished successfully, the water appears to boil with the furiously feeding fish. Other fishermen argue that the fish thus fed will ignore the challenge of a baited hook.

Also illegal are methods involving dynamite or electric shocks to kill large numbers of fish that are then collected rather than caught.

Even the most common pole fishing brought punishment for slaves, because such activity was attributed to laziness. In one folktale, the slave hero, High John the Conqueror, fishes for catfish despite his master's rules against it. John outsmarts his master by saying that he only caught a large catfish to keep it from continually stealing his bait. As any fisherman knows, catfish are accomplished bait-stealers, so the excuse was credible to the suspicious master.

The contemporary catfisherman is likely to have exchanged his cane pole for a graphite one complete with reel and will use monofilament line rather than the cotton or linen that was once used. Still earlier lines were made from twisted horsehair, the number of strands determining its strength.

Despite beliefs to the contrary, catfish do not spend all their time scouring the muddy bottoms of rivers and lakes. Usually they search the areas one to two feet from the bottom, rising to the middle depths or even to the surface in their quest for food. This is why farm-raised catfish are easily trained to come to the top to feed.

During the colder winter months, catfish become lethargic

and retreat to deeper waters. Warming water temperatures bring them upstream in search of food and nesting areas. The male catfish locates the spawning site and encourages a female to lay her eggs there. He then fertilizes them and stands guard until they hatch. To hook the expectant father, the bait must drop right in front of the nest. After the eggs hatch, the parents watch over the fry for another week to ten days. Their parental obligations fulfilled, the adults move back into deeper waters, hungry and eager to bite; but then, being stuck with thousands of offspring for over a week would probably do that to any parent.

An effective variation on pole fishing involves the use of a raft, boat, or tube float. The rig, consisting of sinker and baited hook, is set near the bottom. As the boat is pushed by the current or a breeze, the bait drifts along. Handlining, which uses a line, sinker, and hook, but no pole, can also be done this way. Stories abound about fishermen in boats or floats being "dragged" by large catfish, making one wonder who caught whom. Happily, in the majority of the tales, both the fisherman and the fish get away safely.

Large catfish are being caught in "boils," the wildly turbulent tailrace waters at the bases of dams. A pocket of calm water below the area where the outflow hits the baffle can host a number of big catfish that congregate there to feed. Motor boats, depth detectors, and heavy saltwater tackle are used in "boiling" to hook catfish weighing between forty and ninety-five pounds each.

In January 1990 the Columbus, South Carolina *State Record* reported that fish weighing up to 82 pounds were being caught in Lake Marion's Wilson Dam. "The catfish are so thick," wrote Pat Robertson, "that all that is needed to catch them is to jerk a line fixed with treble hooks through the water."

Trotlines and traps or "baskets" have been popular means of catching catfish since prehistoric times because they can be left unattended for extended periods. These were particularly useful for slaves who could supplement their food allotment without risking punishmnt for taking time away from their assigned tasks. A trotline is simply a submerged cord, anchored at both ends, with baited hooks hanging on smaller lines, called stagings, off the main string.

Jugging is a variation on trotlining, with one end of the line tied to a floating "jug" and the other to a baited hook which bounces along the bottom. Usually several such rigs are thrown into a river and the fishermen follow in boats. When the catfish takes the bait, the jug—usually an empty oil can, plastic bleach bottle, or milk jug—jiggles or goes under until the fish tires. Sometimes a fish is "snagged" along its body on the large treble hooks. The fishermen bring the boat alongside the jug and pull the fish in. This method has been used in southern rivers to catch flatheads weighing well over 100 pounds.

Limb-lining, yet another variation on the trotline, is a fishing technique that involves tying a baited line to a branch overhanging the water. A tree trunk or stump, or any stationary object, can be used. The drop line can be left unattended and checked after several hours. Large fish have been known to break both branches and lines if left too long. In one tall tale, the line is tied instead to the bumper of a pickup truck by someone too lazy to find a tree. The fisherman takes a "catnap" inside and awakens to find his truck and himself being pulled downriver by a large fish.

Nets and seines can bring in great numbers of fish. One antebellum plantation owner near Vidalia, Louisiana, was reportedly so successful with seines that he fed his slaves catfish stew twice a day. In 1812, Audubon reported seeing a slave catching catfish by dipping a "Scoup net" into a swiftly running current, and there are other accounts of slaves drowning while "netting cats."

There are also reports of people being drowned "gigging cats." This method becomes dangerous when a line connected to the end of the spear is tied around the fisherman's waist.

An adventurous way of catching catfish consists of using only the bare hands and is illegal in some states, although Mississippi has a season set aside for it. Called grabbling, graveling, noodling, or simply handgrabbing, this involves reaching into a submerged log or hollow and dragging the astonished catfish out by its gill plate. The poet James Seay gives this colorful description in "Grabbling in Yokna Bottom":

And who would eat a cleaner meat
Must grabble in the hollows of underwater stumps and
    roots.
Must cram his arm and hand beneath the scum
And go by touch where eye cannot reach.
Must seize and bring to light
What scale or slime is touched—
Must in that instant—on touch
Without questioning or reckoning
Grab up what wraps itself cold-blooded
Around flesh or flails the water to froth.
Or else feel the fish slip by.

Experienced "grabber" Frank Selman described the procedure for readers of *Outdoor Life:* "Catfish grabbing is a unique form of fishing where you are the bait and hook." He does admit, however, that for fear of being thought insane "you may wish to keep this particular vice to yourself."

Understandably, this fearless and foolhearty endeavor is undertaken in warm, lazy rivers. One can only speculate what Huckleberry Finn would have thought of it, but it is easy to imagine the fish's reaction. It is one thing to be hauled out of the water while scrounging for something to eat, but quite another to be jerked by the jaw from innocent slumber. I'm not sure polite people do this.

South Mississippi country folk used to make a social event of a practice they called "muddying," according to Rose Budd Stevens in *Along the RFD*. After a dry spell, when the lakes and ponds got low, men, women, and children piled into the biggest wagon, with the wash pot, green onions, and already cooked cornbread, and headed for the nearest water hole. The "muddying" came when the men and children jumped up and down in the water until the mud got so thick the mudcats and other fish had to come to the top for air. Then they all went after the slippery fish. The fish were tossed to the women and old people waiting on the bank to immediately clean and fry the catch.

Another unusual fishing technique is described in a favorite fishing story from *The Yazoo River* by Frank E. Smith. Bob Hooter, grandson of the legendary Mike Hooter of Yazoo County, Mississippi, who was the hero of many humorous sketches written by William C. Hall in the 1850s. Hooter had been disappointed catching only an eel, which he tied to a string near the river bank. At the end of the day, when Bob returned to get the eel, he pulled in a smug eel and a twenty-pound catfish. According to this wonderful tale, when the fish tried to swallow the eel, the eel slipped out through its gills and then coiled the line tightly enough to hook the cat. One hopes that Bob set the helpful eel free.

The lure of catting is not limited to southerners. *The Detroit Free Press* (September 1990) reported the correction of a past error in identifying the record forty-seven-and-a-half pound cat caught in the Maple River as a flathead and not a channel cat. Herb Wilson gave indications of a severe case of catfish fever in describing a trip on the Columbus River in Washington State: "It was a moment I longed to experience ever since I learned there were catfish weighing thirty-five pounds and more in this part of the Northwest."

However it is caught, the catfish does not meekly surrender once brought out of the water. When alarmed, catfish can erect the needlelike spines at the fronts of the dorsal and pectoral fins. These make effective weapons for the furiously squirming would-be captive, and many a fisherman has had success slip from his bleeding fingers. The sting is increased by bacteria on the slime covering the fish's body.

The skirmish is often accompanied by the catfish's loud croaking battle cries, which continue as bleating complaints once the quarry is secured to a stringer. Some people, believing that other catfish hear these croaks as warnings to stay clear of hook-infested waters, will move either themselves or their captive to another spot. Others change baits on the theory that the fish, by these vibrations of his swim bladder, has warned its still-free brethren to "beware of worms."

Even in defeat the catfish will continue to fight, and the sagest advice to anyone preparing to clean a catfish is first to make sure it is dead. Catfish can survive for some time out of water, and the unwary might justifiably wonder whether the notion of "nine lives" pertains more to the aquatic cat than to the land-loving feline to which it usually refers.

THERE'S MORE THAN ONE WAY
TO SKIN A CAT

CATFISH have a way of startling the unwary. One of their most effective shock techniques occurs when the fish is taken home for cleaning. The catfish will appear to be dead, or at least extremely subdued, but upon having a knife thrust into its body will take on new life. It will suddenly squirm furiously and may emit loud croaking complaints at such ill treatment.

Some cleaners have resorted to knocking the fish in the head with a mallet, hammer, or even a rock to silence it. Commercial catfish processors use electric shock to stun the fish before cleaning. Perhaps the most common method for the average fisherman is to quickly force a long knife or ice pick either into the spine right at the base of the head or into the brain, between and slightly behind the eyes. If this operation is successful, the knife will also serve to hold the fish to a board, fence post, or tree for cleaning.

Because catfish do not have scales, cleaning them is not the scraping process it is with most fish. Instead, catfish are skinned, and, as the old expression goes, there really is more than one way to skin a cat.

Some people, having problems skinning something that seems to be watching the whole process, cut off the head and then hold the fish in hand while cleaning, or attach it to the board by the tail or near the top of its body.

A regular fish scaling board is sometimes used, with the clip holding the tail. The cleaner cuts a shallow slit crosswise just below the tail and peels the skin off with pliers, working towards the head. Whether the head and fins are removed first or last is a matter of personal preference.

Some people gut the catfish before skinning it, although others leave the fish ungutted until the end on the theory that the fish "holds together better." In this case, a cut is sometimes made just behind the head. Then, after the fish is skinned, the head is pulled downward until the backbone snaps and the head and entrails can be pulled out together.

Many remove the dorsal and pectoral fins first with a pair of pliers or wire-cutters, because the punctures caused by the needle-like spines sting badly and are easily infected.

Pliers are generally used to clean catfish, since the skin is rubbery and adheres tightly to the meaty flesh. In one method, the cleaner begins by grasping the fins and pulling sharply downward toward the tail, peeling large areas of skin along the way. Or a person may make a shallow slit down the full length of the back, cutting around the fins. Then the pliers are used to remove the skin, usually from head to tail. When the process is done well, the skin is taken off in large pieces, and the clean flesh is left intact. The head and fins are removed last.

Small catfish are sometimes dipped into boiling water, or boiling water may be poured over them. This not only kills the fish but supposedly makes them easier to skin.

Especially large fish may be held by the head while a diamond-shaped cut is made on the belly from the pectoral to the pelvic fins. Another cut is made on the back, from behind the head down the sides to the pectoral fins. Then the skin is sliced from a point just behind the head around the dorsal fin. The cleaner uses pliers to grasp the fish's skin at the neck and pulls it sharply toward the tail. The fins, head, and entrails are removed last. The largest fish have to be decapitated with a hammer and a big knife or cleaver.

As the final step in any skinning method, the fish is rinsed in clean water inside and out, so that all vestiges of skin and internal workings are completely removed.

Small catfish—pan-sized—are usually cooked whole, but the

Whole, dressed catfish have the head, tail, and fins removed.

Fillets are the boned sides of the fish.

Fillets can be cut into strips.

Larger catfish can be cut crosswise, into steaks.

larger catfish can be filleted or cut crosswise into steaks. Catfish have prominent bones and are easier to eat than most fish with the bones still in.

Commercial processors use an assembly line method to clean catfish. The fish are brought into the plant in tanks and an electrical current is shot through the whole tank to stun the fish seconds before the skinning begins. The head is removed by spinning motorized blades. Then the belly of the fish is slit and the guts suctioned out. Cold water lowers the fish's body temperature before it goes through the assembly line to be skinned. Next, the fish are sorted by size. Small fish are left whole, while medium-sized and large fish are filleted or cut into steaks. Finally, the pieces are individually quick-frozen. The whole process, from the stun to the deep freeze, takes less than ten minutes, so that the fish retain their "just caught" taste.

FARM-RAISED CATFISH

THE economic possibilities of raising catfish in commercial ponds, such as the ones already being used for trout,
began to be seriously explored by southern agricultural experiment stations in the mid- to late 1950s. Although some of
these early reports dealt with bullheads, the studies quickly began to concentrate on the channel catfish. By the 1960s there
were commercial catfish ponds in Arkansas, Alabama, Mississippi, and Texas, among other southern states. Arkansas took an
early lead and maintained that position until about 1965, when
the cotton and soybean fields in west-central Mississippi began
increasingly to be converted to commercial catfish ponds.

Since its beginnings in 1975, catfish farming has expanded

rapidly, particularly in that part of Mississippi known as the Delta, the flatlands between the Mississippi and Yazoo Rivers. In 1976, there were only about thirty-three major catfish producers in America, with 5,882 acres in all. Now approximately 161,000 acres in 16 states are dedicated to catfish ponds. Over 94,000 acres are located in Mississippi, which produces about 75 percent of the nation's domestically produced catfish.

Much of the phenomenal growth is a result of an increasingly health-conscious public, but it is also largely due to the successful marketing skills of the industry itself. The Catfish Institute, formed in 1986, is supported by Mississippi processors and feed mills and actively promotes catfish as a healthy and tasty product. Advertisements placed in newspapers and magazines around the country "In praise of the lowly catfish" state:

> *Admittedly, when Mother Nature—with the latter-day help of some folks in Mississippi—created the Catfish, it wasn't to win beauty contests. No. The variety known as Mississippi Prime was endowed with far more important qualities: A fine, firm texture and delicate flavor. Flesh that always cooks tender and flaky, never mushy. A fish rich in nutrients, virtually without cholesterol and fat. In short, looks aside, the perfect fish.*

Catfish Farmers of America, proudly touted as "America's largest aquaculture organization," has members in 35 states. Formed in 1968, it is an association of farm-raised catfish producers, suppliers, processors, and marketers. It provides continuing education programs, government relations, and meetings to promote the growth of the industry. It also produces its own trade publication, *The Catfish Journal*.

Production of the fish has increased dramatically, with over 360 million pounds reported by major processors in this country in 1990 and just over 3 million pounds imported, primarily from Brazil.

In the Mississippi Delta, catfish are raised in "levee ponds," constructed on the heavy clay soils. Dirt is pushed from what will be the bottom of the pond to surround it with levees, which are usually fifteen to thirty feet wide at the top. These ponds vary greatly in size and shape but average about seventeen acres of water on about twenty acres of land. Each acre can easily support from 4,000 to 8,000 fish. Some farmers, however, raise many more.

The pond bottoms are not level, as might be expected, but slope down to only about five feet so that gravity can drain them into nearby canals or ditches when necessary. The average water depth tends to be only about four feet. Although the area tends to get abundant rainfall, additional water must be pumped in from wells. The water quality greatly affects the quality of the fish and is carefully regulated.

Some farms specialize, producing, for instance, only fingerlings, which will be sold to other catfish farmers to raise to processing size. Many farms, though, have some of everything. Brood fish are kept in separate ponds and spawn in late spring and early summer, producing 2,000 to 4,000 eggs per pound of the female's body weight. The eggs, which are in a jelly-like mass called a "spawn," are moved to the hatchery. The hatchery generally operates from early May through July and is where the catfish are allowed to hatch. The "fry," as baby fish are called, begin to eat on the third day but are held in the hatchery for five to fifteen days before being transferred to a nursery pond, where they stay through the summer and fall, growing to about one-twentieth to fifteen-twentieths of a pound. These "fingerlings" are then placed in production or food-fish ponds, where they grow to a weight of one to two pounds in an average of eighteen to twenty-four months.

A study conducted by Dr. John Waldrup of Mississippi State University showed that production costs rise dramatically for large fish, which bring less return per pound at the processors. For example, a catfish sold at thirty months will cost 20 percent more than one sold at eighteen months. A fish held until the forty-second month will increase the grower's cost by 56 percent. Fish are generally held because they are "off-flavor" and cannot be sold, because the grower is waiting for higher prices or because there's no market demand.

Processors employ "tasters" as part of their quality control to insure against "off-flavor" fish. Before a farmer's fish can be processed, samples must be presented for testing. An "off-flavor" fish causes the rejection of an entire pond of fish and the farmer cannot sell any until he solves the problem, which he usually does by working with the water.

The fish are harvested with large-meshed seines which allow the smaller fish to slip back into the pond for further growth. Fingerlings are then added to replace the fish removed.

Catfish are moved in tank trucks to the processing plant, where they are lifted out with a hydraulic lift. The fish are stunned with an electric current, decapitated, gutted, skinned, washed, and quick-frozen in a process that takes only minutes. The heads and entrails, used for animal feed as well as fertilizer, are put on transport trucks.

In 1989 a study was done by the Mississippi Agricultural and Forestry Experiment Station at Mississippi State University to determine the demographic and attitudinal characteristics of catfish consumers. The results were surprising.

Although catfish have the reputation of being a "poor man's fish" eaten primarily by southerners, the researchers found in a survey of 3,600 households nationwide that more catfish consumers stated that they lived in suburban areas than in cities or rural areas, and that the head of household was in a professional occupation. As might be expected, three-fourths of all southerners surveyed could be classified as catfish consumers, but they are not alone. The north central areas of the United States, including the Northern Plains states and the Midwest, ate more catfish than any other fish. The *Nation's Restaurant News* reported in 1989: "Catfish is no longer just a Southern Specialty. American Southwest, East, and West operations feature it . . . Consumers who might never sample catfish in its home territory can now order it in dining establishments around the country." Consumers in the $20,000-to-$30,000-per-year income bracket had the highest percentage of catfish consumption, while the lowest percentage was in the less-than-$10,000 bracket. When asked to name their favorite fish and seafood, people placed catfish third behind shrimp and lobster, but ahead of crab, scallops, flounder, cod, and salmon.

Still, the per capita consumption of catfish is less than one pound per person per year, compared to poultry, which is sixty pounds per person; so there is still room for growth for the South's favorite fish.

COOKING CATFISH

ALMOST everyone would agree that the traditional southern method to cook catfish is to fry it. It is when the details of that endeavor are outlined that peaceful negotiation tends to break down.

Only a discussion of the "correct" way to fry chicken can provoke more disagreement. That problem can be easily solved once it is realized that "Mama's way" is the "right way." Some people just happen to have had the wrong mamas. That cannot be helped.

The trouble with catfish, though, is that daddies fry them too. Grandmas, grandpas, aunts, uncles, and cousins twice removed all fry catfish. Neighbors, friends, coworkers and even strangers have done it. And all are absolutely certain that their method is best, most traditional, and maybe even God-given. The solution to this puzzle is also simple. Do it your own way, and do not waste time arguing with the misguided about it.

Different methods, not necessarily your own correct one, will be discussed here. Please understand that this is done only in the interest of harmony, and that a mention here does not necessarily constitute an endorsement for any method other than yours.

Much like the never-ending chicken controversy, the conflict begins with how to prepare the fish for cooking. There are those who will only prepare and eat fillets averaging three-to-five ounces each. The notion is that anything smaller is not worth the effort and anything larger does not "fry up" evenly.

Take careful note of the terminology. Catfish are "fried up," usually in units known as "messes," although "bunch of" is also acceptable. The distinction seems to be that although it is correct to use "fry" when talking about the method, the actual procedure requires "frying up."

Some people insist on the smaller pan-sized variety, with the actual size being relatively dependent upon the dimensions of the utensil being used. In this case, the fish are fried whole—without the head, of course, because a catfish's head would take up a sizeable portion of the pan.

Other catfish epicureans prefer steaks cut cross-wise from the larger catfish. These are generally rather uniform in size and fit in the pan or fryer nicely.

The real argument begins, however, with what to do next. Some dip the fish in buttermilk, with or without beaten egg, to make a crispy crust, while others assert that this results instead in a "pasty" crust.

Difficult as it may be for many southerners to believe, there are people who, before frying the catfish, inexplicably dredge it only in regular white, all-purpose flour, without any cornmeal, even when they have plenty on the shelf. The flour is seasoned with salt, lemon pepper, garlic, cayenne and/or paprika, and perhaps even a dash of dry mustard.

The more common (i.e., "correct") method utilizes corn-meal. There is, however, substantial disagreement over the proper type of cornmeal to be used, the finer white or the coarser yellow or a combination of both, and whether a bit of all-purpose white flour should be included in the dredging mixture to make the meal adhere more evenly to the fish.

Spices are also a source of dissension. There are numerous proponents of the "salt and pepper only" school, while others add a variety of flavorings including lemon pepper, cayenne, seasoned salt, garlic, paprika, and/or onion salt.

There are also several commercial "fish fry" mixtures on the market. Some cooks swear by these and others at them. Others compromise by using part cornmeal (of whatever color) and part "fish fry."

Whatever the decision, the fish, either dipped first in buttermilk and/or beaten egg, or not, is coated with the mixture. At this point, some people recommend setting the fish in the refrigerator for a few minutes, while waiting for the grease to get hot, so that the crust can "set." This minor point does not seem to engender bloodshed, although there is some speculation that this action is included primarily by cooks who are forever tidying up between steps.

The type of grease utilized is the next area of disagreement. It is important to realize that the term "grease" is used generically to include all kinds of oil, lard, and shortening.

The traditional grease for everything was pork lard. As Dr. John S. Wilson of Columbus, Georgia, complained in an 1860 issue of *Godey's Lady's Book,* people "indeed fried everything that is fryable, or that will stick together long enough to undergo the delightful process . . . hogs' lard is the very oil that moves the machinery of life, and they would as soon think of dispensing with tea, coffee, or tobacco . . . as with the essence of hog."

In addition to the lard and shortening, cooks may choose from a variety of oils. These include peanut, corn, sunflower, and safflower oils, as well as regular vegetable oil.

The type of utensil used is the next source of argument, with some insisting on that irreplaceable southern cookery tool, the "big black skillet." Loss of this implement is considered catastrophic, and many a meal has been delayed by its misplacement. Substitutions are not acceptable.

The less tradition-minded, however, may succumb to using any other large frying pan or even an electric skillet, though it is socially unacceptable to admit to this culinary deviation publicly.

Many people do not use frying pans or skillets at all but insist instead on deep fryers, some of which are made specifically for frying fish.

Whatever the implement, there is little disagreement that it is of great importance to get the grease hot enough before frying the fish. There is some room for discussion about how to define that elusive "just right" temperature. One of the more common methods is to drop a piece of cornmeal into the sizzling liquid. If the cornmeal "dances," the grease is ready.

A standard accompaniment for catfish is hushpuppies, preferably fried in the same grease as the fish. Coleslaw and french fried potatoes are also often served. Additional side dishes might include such regional favorites as greens, pickled onions, fried pickles, or grits. In early eighteenth century Pennsylvania, catfish and waffle suppers were popular.

The final argument develops over the condiments served with catfish. Some demand tartar sauce or Tabasco. Others want lemon or malt vinegar. A few request syrup. Cooking authority Craig Claiborne insists on ketchup, saying, "Deep-fried catfish without ketchup is like a hot dog without mustard." The ketchup can come straight from the bottle or be mixed with Tabasco, Worcestershire sauce, or other flavorings. There are some, however, who believe that fried catfish require nothing more than a hearty appetite.

One of the most common methods of cooking catfish historically did not involve frying at all. Instead, catfish were cooked in a stew or "muddle." One early recipe has tomatoes, onion, fatback, salt and pepper, but apparently other ingredients, such as okra, potatoes, and carrots, were added as available. More recent concoctions include ketchup and hot sauce.

Now that channel cats are being raised and marketed commercially, more sophisticated dishes are being prepared. Catfish almondine, stuffed catfish, blackened catfish, catfish souffle, and numerous other recipes have been developed. Catfish are baked, braised, boiled, barbequed, casseroled, steamed and stuffed. At St. Cloud's in Boston, catfish is served pan-fried with adobe spices and wrapped in corn husks. In New York's East Village, it is pan-fried with mashed sweet potatoes, and at Trump's in Los Angeles, catfish is served with a black bean sauce.

There has even been a catfish sausage developed, low in fat and calories for the health-conscious consumer. A National Farm-Raised Catfish Cooking Contest, which was held annually, fostered the discovery of new, innovative ways of preparing the South's favorite fish. Most of the recipes included in this book were winners in that contest.

Largely due to the marketing skills and constantly improving product of the farm-raised catfish industry, this southern native is achieving national and international culinary recognition. Catfish are being served at diplomatic functions as well as local fund-raising fish fries, and are as likely to be on the menus of high-level summit meetings as the Friday night special at small town diners. As Mark Twain accurately maintained, "The catfish is a plenty good enough fish for anybody."

RECIPES

APPETIZERS

Pasta with Catfish and Artichokes

Serves 8

2 4–5 ounce catfish fillets
3 tablespoons butter
1 cup sliced artichoke hearts
1 red pepper, cut julienne strips
1 carrot, cut julienne strips
1 zucchini, cut julienne strips
2/3 cup heavy cream (or milk, if preferred)
1/4 pound angel hair pasta or vermicelli
1/2 cup grated Parmesan cheese
1/4 teaspoon ground nutmeg

Cut catfish in half crosswise and slice into thin strips. Saute catfish in melted butter; add artichokes, red pepper, carrot strips, and zucchini. Cook until tender. Stir in heavy cream. Keep warm. Meanwhile cook pasta according to package directions and drain. Toss well with cream mixture and cheese. Sprinkle with nutmeg and serve immediately.

Ceviche

Serves 8

2 4–5 ounce catfish fillets
½ pound bay scallops
½ cup fresh lemon juice
½ cup fresh lime juice
½ cup chopped fresh mint (or 2 tablespoons dried)
¼ teaspoon hot pepper sauce
¾ cup chopped tomatoes
½ cup chopped red onion
Lettuce leaves
1 ripe avocado
Mint sprigs

Slice fillets lengthwise and then crosswise into ¼-inch thick slices. Combine catfish, scallops, lemon juice, lime juice, mint and hot pepper sauce in a shallow non-metallic container. Cover tightly and refrigerate from 8–24 hours. When ready to serve, drain catfish and scallops. Add tomatoes and red onion; toss well. Peel and slice avocado. Arrange ceviche on plates lined with lettuce. Garnish with avocado slices and mint sprigs.

Catfish Sticks

Serves 8

4 4–5 *ounce catfish fillets*
½ *cup yellow cornmeal*
1 *teaspoon chili powder*
½ *teaspoon salt*
Tartar sauce, lemon wedges or other
  condiments
½ *teaspoon oregano*
⅓ *cup milk*
1 *egg*
Vegetable oil

Cut catfish into 1- x 4-inch sticks. Combine cornmeal, chili powder, salt and oregano; mix well. Beat together milk and egg. Dip catfish sticks into milk mixture and then into cornmeal. Pour oil to a depth of 1 inch in a deep fryer or heavy pan. Fry sticks in small batches until golden brown. Drain on paper towels. Serve immediately with tartar sauce and lemon wedges.

Catfish Golden Nuggets

Serves 6

2 pounds catfish fillets
1 cup all-purpose flour
½ cup cornmeal
1 ½ teaspoon seasoned salt
1 teaspoon baking powder
¼ teaspoon lemon pepper
2 eggs beaten
1 ¼ cups buttermilk
¼ cup finely chopped pecans or almonds
Oil for frying
Sauce

Cut fillets into pieces approximately 1 ½ x 1 ¼ inches. In a large bowl, sift together flour, cornmeal, seasoned salt, baking powder, and lemon pepper. Add eggs and milk; blend into a smooth batter. Stir in pecans or almonds. Dip catfish in batter, let excess batter drip off and place on wax paper. Fry in deep fat for 3 to 5 minutes, until golden brown and catfish flakes easily. Drain on absorbant paper. Serve with Zippy Cream 'N' Pickle Sauce. [Linda's note: Kathy Starr's Candied Wing Sauce goes great.]

Zippy Cream 'n' Pickle Sauce

Makes approximately 2 cups sauce

1 cup sour cream
¾ cup relish sandwich spread
2 tablespoons pickle relish
2 tablespoons finely chopped onion
1 tablespoon chopped parsley
1 tablespoon lemon juice
1 teaspoon dried dill weed
½ teaspoon cream-style prepared horseradish
3 or 4 dashes Tabasco

Combine all ingredients. Chill for 30 minutes to blend flavors.

Kathy Starr's Candied Wing Sauce

2 cups ribbon cane syrup
½ cup hot sauce
¾ stick butter

Mix syrup, butter, and hot sauce in a pan over medium heat, stirring and cooking until bubbly, about 8 to 10 minutes.

Catfish Appetizer Nuggets

Makes about 6 dozen

2 *pounds nuggets or fillets, cubed*
1 *cup finely crushed round cheese crackers*
½ *cup Parmesan cheese*
½ *teaspoon salt*
¼ *teaspoon pepper*
½ *cup melted butter*
⅓ *cup sesame seeds*

Combine cracker crumbs, cheese, sesame seeds, salt and pepper in small bowl and set aside. Dip fish cubes into butter and roll in crumb mixture. Place fish ½ inch apart on foil-lined baking sheets. Bake uncovered at 400 degrees for 20 minutes or until golden brown. Serve immediately with Sour Cream Blue Cheese Dip.

Sour Cream Blue Cheese Dip

1 *8-ounce carton sour cream*
2 *tablespoons crumbed blue cheese*
¼ *cup finely chopped onion*
¼ *teaspoon salt*

Combine all ingredients. Cover and refrigerate until serving.

Catfish and Fruit Salad

2 pounds fillets, in 1-inch chunks
2 cups boiling water
½ cup diced onion
¼ cup lemon juice
1 teaspoon salt
1 chilled medium cantaloupe
5 ¼ ounces pineapple bits, drained
11 ounces mandarin orange bits, drained
1 cup diagonally sliced celery
Salad greens
Fresh strawberries, garnish
Celery seed dressing

In a 10-inch skillet, combine water, onion, lemon and salt. Bring
mixture to a boil. Add fish. Cover and simmer for 5 to 8 minutes
or until fish is done. Drain well. Place fish in a bowl. Pour one-
half celery seed dressing over, cover and refrigerate until well
chilled. Slice half the melon into 6-inch rings and the remaining
half into chunks. Arrange melon rings on lettuce. Lightly toss
the fish mixture, fruit, and celery. Fill melon rings with salad
mixture. Garnish with fresh strawberries. Serve with remaining
dressing.

Celery Seed Dressing

½ cup honey
½ cup red wine vinegar
⅓ cup salad oil
3 tablespoons sugar
¾ teaspoon dry mustard
½ teaspoon paprika
½ teaspoon celery seed
½ teaspoon salt

Combine all ingredients. Mix well and chill until ready to serve.

Catfish Cocktail

Serves 6

1 pound catfish fillets, cubed
2 cups chicken broth
8-ounce bottle lime juice, chilled
⅓ cup thinly sliced celery
6 tablespoons chopped purple onion
2 tablespoons chopped green pepper
1 tablespoon chopped fresh parsley
1 cup chili sauce, chilled
2 teaspoons prepared horseradish

Tabasco sauce to taste
1 avocado, peeled and diced into ½-inch cubes
Lettuce, parsley, lime slices

In a medium pan bring chicken broth to a boil; reduce heat and add fish. Cook fish for 3 to 5 minutes until done. Drain well. Place fish in a glass bowl. Pour lime juice over the fish, cover and refrigerate at least 30 minutes. In a large bowl combine celery, onion, pepper, parsley, chili sauce, horseradish, and Tabasco. Drain fish. Add fish cubes and avocado to sauce mixture and toss. Serve on lettuce or in tomato cups. Garnish with parsley sprigs and lime slices.

Catfish Party Mousse

2 pounds catfish fillets or nuggets
2 quarts water
¼ cup liquid crab & shrimp boil
2 tablespoons salt
2 envelopes unflavored gelatin
½ cup cold water
8 ounces cream cheese, softened
8 ounces sour cream
1 can cream of mushroom soup

3 hard boiled eggs, chopped
1 cup finely chopped onion
½ cup finely chopped celery
½ cup chopped green pepper
½ cup chopped pimiento
1 tablespoon lemon juice
1 teaspoon Worcestershire
½ teaspoon salt
⅛ teaspoon white pepper
Salad greens
Assorted crackers

Bring water, crab boil and 2 tablespoons salt to a boil. Add fish and return to a boil; reduce heat and cook for 8 to 10 minutes until done. Drain fish and flake into small pieces. Combine gelatin with ½ cup cold water. Let stand five minutes. Dissolve over hot water. In a mixing bowl combine cream cheese, sour cream, and soup. Blend until smooth. Add dissolved gelatin. Add fish flakes, eggs, onions, celery, green pepper, pimiento, lemon juice, Worcestershire sauce, salt and pepper. Mix well. Pour mixture into a 1 ½-quart mold. Refrigerate until set. Unmold on salad greens. Serve with crackers.

Catfish Mousse

1 can cream of shrimp soup
8 ounces cream cheese, softened
1 envelope unflavored gelatin
1 4–5 ounce catfish fillet
1 tablespoon lemon juice
½ cup finely chopped celery
¼ cup finely chopped onion
1 cup mayonnaise
1 tablespoon Worcestershire
Crackers or vegetables

Combine soup and cream cheese; bring to a boil, stirring until smooth. Sprinkle gelatin over soup; refrigerate 15 minutes. Place catfish fillet in boiling salted water. Cover and simmer 10 minutes or until fish flakes easily. Drain and flake catfish. Combine cooked catfish, soup mixture, celery, onion, mayonnaise, Worcestershire sauce and lemon juice. Chill until thickened. Pipe with pastry bag onto crackers or vegetables.

Creamy Catfish Dip

Makes about 3 cups

1 *pound boiled and flaked catfish*
½ *pint small curd cottage cheese*
½ *pint sour cream*
½ *cup shredded raw carrot*
¼ *cup chopped dill pickle, well drained*
2 *tablespoons chopped pimiento*
1 *teaspoon horseradish*
¼ *teaspoon salt*
Chopped parsley
Assorted raw vegetables, chips and/or crackers

Combine cottage cheese, sour cream, pickle, pimiento, horse-radish, and salt; mix well. Stir in flaked fish. Chill several hours before serving. Sprinkle with parsley and serve with raw vegetables, chips, or crackers.

Catfish-Tomato Cups

Serves 6

3 *cups boiled and flaked catfish*
1 *cup chopped celery*
⅔ *cup chopped green pepper*
¼ *cup chopped onion*
2 *teaspooons curry powder*

1 teaspoon salt
1 cup mayonnaise or salad dressing
6 tomatoes
Salad greens
Chopped parsley to garnish

Combine all ingredients except tomatoes, salad greens, and parsley. Toss lightly. Chill. Cut each tomato into 5 or 6 sections almost to stem and spread open slightly. Fill each with catfish salad. Garnish with chopped parsley. Serve on salad greens.

Catfish Salad

Serves 4

2 4-ounce catfish fillets, cubed
1 red pepper, roasted, and cut into strips
1 small red onion, sliced
1 tablespoon fresh chopped dill or ½ teaspoon
  dried dill
¼ cup olive oil
¼ cup red wine vinegar
2 cups torn romaine lettuce
1 head Boston lettuce, torn
4 strips fried bacon, crumbled
3 ounces Blue cheese, crumbled
Salt and pepper to taste

Place catfish cubes in skillet and add water to cover. Simmer 5–7 minutes or until catfish flakes easily. Drain. In large bowl, combine catfish cubes, pepper strips, onion rings, dill, oil and vinegar. Cover and marinate at least one hour. Just before serving, toss with lettuce and blue cheese. Salt and pepper to taste.

Smoked Catfish Log

Makes about 2 cups

> *2 cups smoked catfish (recipe in main dishes)*
> *1 tablespoon lemon juice*
> *1 teaspoon horseradish*
> *¼ teaspoon salt*
> *2 tablespoons chopped parsley*
> *8 ounces cream cheese, softened*
> *2 teaspoons grated onion*
> *½ cup chopped nuts*
> *Assorted crackers*

Flake fish. Combine cheese, lemon juice, onion, horseradish and smoked fish, mixing well. Chill for several hours. Combine pecans and parsley. Shape smoked fish mixture into a log and roll in nut mixture.

SOUPS AND STEWS

Catfish and Broccoli Chowder

Serves 6

1 pound catfish fillets, cubed
3 slices bacon
1 cup chopped onion
1 clove garlic, minced
3 cups chicken broth
10 ounces chopped broccoli, thawed
3 ounces cream cheese, softened and cubed
¼ teaspoon salt
⅛ teaspoon white pepper
1 cup heavy cream, room temperature
3 tablespoons flour
Paprika

Cook bacon in heavy Dutch oven over medium heat until crisp.
Set aside bacon; crumble, reserve 2 tablespoons drippings. Cook

onion and garlic in drippings for 5 minutes or until tender. Add broth, broccoli, salt and pepper. Cook until broccoli is crisp tender. Add fish cubes, cover and simmer for 10 minutes or until fish and broccoli are done. Combine cream and flour until mixture is smooth. Add to hot mixture gradually and cook over low heat, stirring continuously, until mixture is thick and hot enough to serve. Garnish with crumbled bacon and paprika.

Catfish and Shrimp Soup

Serves 8

2 tablespoons olive oil
2 cups chopped onion
2 cloves garlic, minced
1 can (28 ounces) tomatoes
3 tablespoons tomato paste
1 bay leaf
4 cups water
1 cup dry white wine
8-ounce bottle clam juice
½ pound medium shelled shrimp
2 4–5 ounce catfish fillets, cubed
½ teaspoon salt
¼ teaspoon pepper
Coriander (or parsley)
Lemon slices

In a large soup pot, heat oil and saute onion and garlic until onion is transparent. Add tomatoes, tomato paste, and bay leaf. Cover and simmer 25 minutes. Add water, wine, and clam juice. Simmer uncovered for 45 minutes. Add shrimp, catfish, salt and pepper. Cook 10 minutes or until catfish flakes easily. Remove bay leaf. Garnish each serving with chopped coriander and lemon slices.

Catfish Chowder

Serves 10

4 tablespoons butter
1 cup chopped onion
½ cup sliced celery
4 cups peeled, diced potatoes
4 cups chicken broth
2 cups water
2 cans (each 8 ounces) corn, drained
4 4–5 ounce catfish fillets, cubed
½ cup flour
1 cup milk
Salt and pepper to taste
Chopped parsley (optional)

Heat 1 tablespoon butter in large stock pot. Saute onion and celery until tender. Add potatoes, chicken broth, and water. Cover and simmer 20 minutes. Add corn and catfish. Simmer 15 minutes or until catfish flakes easily. Melt remaining 3 table-spoons of butter. Beat butter and flour together until smooth. Gradually whisk into soup. Simmer 5–7 minutes. Stir in milk and heat thoroughly. Season with salt and pepper to taste. Garnish with parsley.

Catfish Gumbo

Serves 10

¼ *cup vegetable oil*
1 cup chopped celery
1 cup chopped green pepper
1 cup chopped onion
2 cloves garlic, chopped
4 cups beef broth
1 16-ounce can tomatoes
Cooked rice (optional)
10 ounces frozen sliced okra
½ *teaspoon thyme*
1 bay leaf
½ *teaspoon cayenne pepper*
½ *teaspoon oregano*
1 teaspoon salt
4 4–5 ounce catfish fillets, cubed

Heat oil in large stock pot. Saute celery, green pepper, onion, and garlic. Add beef broth, tomatoes, okra, thyme, bay leaf, cayenne pepper, oregano, and salt. Cover and simmer 30 minutes. Add catfish and continue simmering 15 minutes or until catfish flakes easily. Remove bay leaf. Serve over cooked rice, if desired.

Catfish Soup Von Friedricks

Serves 8

2 pounds catfish nuggets
3 cans (10 ¾ ounce) chicken broth
½ cup water
½ cup grated carrots
½ cup chopped celery
1 cup chopped green onions
1 medium onion, chopped
½ cup butter or margarine
1 cup flour
3 soup cans milk
1 ⅓ cups cheese spread
½ teaspoon salt
1 teaspoon black pepper
¼ teaspoon cayenne pepper

1 tablespoon prepared mustard
¼ cup sherry

Boil catfish in 1 ½ cans chicken broth and ½ cup water for 10 minutes and set aside. Boil carrots, celery, and green onions in remaining broth for 5 minutes and set aside. Saute onion in butter until tender. Add flour and blend well. Add milk and cook until mixture thickens. Add cheese, salt, pepper, and cayenne pepper. Stir in mustard and boiled vegetables. Cook an additional 5 minutes. Add catfish mixture and sherry. Heat thoroughly.

Morocan Catfish Couscous

¼ cup slivered almonds
2 tablespoons olive oil
1 medium onion, chopped
2 cloves garlic, minced
2 medium carrots, cut diagonally
1 small red bell pepper, cut into strips
1 medium zucchini, cut into strips
1 teaspoon ground coriander
½ teaspoon cayenne pepper
1 ¾ cups chicken stock
2 cups water
4 4–5 ounce catfish fillets, cut into strips

1 cup canned chickpeas, drained
1 cup of couscous or rice

Place almonds on baking sheet and toast at 350 degrees 8 to 10 minutes until golden brown; set aside. Heat oil in large heavy skillet, add onions, and cook over medium heat until softened. Add garlic, carrots, peppers, seasonings, chicken broth and water. Bring to a boil and cook 5 minutes. Reduce heat and add catfish, chickpeas, and zucchini. Simmer 12 to 15 minutes until catfish flakes easily. Prepare couscous (a semolina cereal native to North Africa) or rice according to package directions. Mound couscous or rice on a large platter, making a well in the center. Fill with catfish and vegetables, reserving some of the broth, and sprinkle with toasted almonds. Serve remaining broth separately to be spooned over individual servings. If preferred, couscous or rice can be served separately with guests mixing own bowl.

MAIN DISHES

Catfish Caribbean

Serves 4

2 tablespoons butter
1/4 cup chopped green pepper
4 tablespoons chopped onion
1/4 cup chopped toasted almonds
1/2 cup fresh bread crumbs
1/4 teaspoon oregano
4 tablespoons lime juice
1 bay leaf
1 tablespoon chopped coriander or parsley
1/2 teaspoon salt
4 4–5 ounce catfish fillets
2 cups water
2 cloves garlic, crushed
1 teaspoon red pepper flakes
Lime peel to garnish

Saute 2 tablespoons onion and the green pepper in butter. Add almonds, bread crumbs, oregano, 1 tablespoon lime juice, coriander and salt; mix well. Spoon filling down center of each fillet. Roll up and secure with toothpicks. In shallow baking pan, combine 2 tablespoons onion, water, garlic, bay leaf, red pepper and 3 tablespoons lime juice. Place catfish in pan. Bake in 400 degree oven for 30-35 minutes until catfish flakes easily. Remove catfish to serving platter and garnish with lime peel.

Catfish Meuniere

Serves 4

¼ *cup milk*
1 egg
⅓ *cup flour*
½ *teaspoon salt*
½ *teaspoon cayenne pepper*
4 4–5 ounce catfish fillets
½ *cup butter*
¼ *cup vegetable oil*
2 tablespoons lemon juice
1 tablespoon chopped parsley
½ *teaspoon Worcestershire*
Parsley and lemon to garnish

In shallow pan, combine milk and egg. In another shallow pan, combine flour, salt, and cayenne pepper. Dip catfish fillets in milk mixture and then flour mixture, shaking off excess. Heat 4 tablespoons butter and the oil in large skillet. Add fillets and cook until golden, turning only once. Meanwhile melt remaining 4 tablespoons butter. Combine with lemon juice, parsley and Worcestershire sauce. Transfer fillets to serving plate. Pour butter over catfish and garnish with parsley and lemon.

Catfish Aurore

Serves 4

¼ *cup heavy cream*
¾ *teaspoon buttermilk*
¼ *cup white wine*
8 *ounces clam juice*
3 *teaspoons fresh thyme leaves or* 1 ½ *teaspoon dried*
1 *clove garlic, minced*
4 4–5 *ounce catfish fillets*
1 *tablespoon olive oil*
⅛ *teaspoon crushed red pepper flakes*
8 *plum tomatoes, peeled, seeded, and chopped*

On previous night, combine cream and buttermilk. Cover and let stand overnight at room temperature to make creme fraiche.

In large skillet combine white wine, clam juice, 1 teaspoon thyme leaves, and catfish fillets. Cover and simmer for 5 to 10 minutes, or until catfish flakes easily. Move the fillets with a slotted spoon to a warm serving plate. In a medium skillet, saute garlic in olive oil and red pepper flakes. When garlic is golden brown, add chopped tomatoes and 2 teaspoons thyme. Simmer for 15 minutes. Remove from heat and stir in cream and buttermilk mixture. Serve sauce with catfish and garnish with fresh or dried thyme.

Catfish en Papillote

Serves 4

1 tablespoon soy sauce
3 tablespoons dry sherry
1 clove garlic, minced
2 tablespoons chopped scallions
¼ teaspoon ground ginger
4 4–5 ounce catfish fillets, cubed
1 red pepper, cut into strips
*2 ounces thinly sliced ham, cut in julienne
    strips*
8 lemon slices

In medium bowl, combine soy sauce, sherry, garlic, scallions, ginger, and cubed catfish. Preheat oven to 450 degrees. Cut 4

1-foot-square pieces of parchment paper or aluminum foil. Fold paper into triangles; open and place catfish inside. Top with red pepper strips, ham and 2 slices of lemon. Spoon sauce over mixture. Fold edges of paper into triangles; crimp edges to seal tightly. Place on a baking sheet and bake 10–12 minutes or until catfish flakes easily. Remove from baking sheet and open paper.

Pecan Catfish

Serves 4

> *2 tablespoons milk*
> *3 tablespoons Dijon mustard*
> *4 4–5 ounce catfish fillets*
> *1 cup ground pecans*

In a small bowl, combine milk and Dijon mustard. Dip fillets into mixture and then into ground pecans, shaking off excess. Place on greased baking sheet. Oven fry at 500 degrees for 10–12 minutes or until catfish flakes easily.

Smoky Broiled Catfish

Serves 4

3 tablespoons soy sauce
1 tablespoon lemon juice
¼ teaspoon garlic powder
2 teaspoons liquid smoke
4 4–5 ounce catfish fillets (or whole catfish)

In a small bowl, combine everything but catfish. Preheat broiler pan for 5 minutes. Coat pan with shortening spray. Place catfish on pan and brush with mixture. Broil 3 inches from heat for 4 to 6 minutes, basting occasionally. If using whole catfish, broil catfish for 3 minutes on each side, basting occasionally.

Catfish with Mustard and Creme Sauce

Serves 4

1 cup heavy cream (or ½ cup each lowfat milk and white wine)
1 tablespoon Dijon mustard
½ teaspoon ground pepper
4 4–5 ounce catfish fillets
1 tablespoon lemon juice
Chopped parsley to garnish

In large skillet, combine cream, mustard, pepper, and catfish.
Bring to a boil. Reduce heat and cover; cook 10−15 minutes or
until catfish flakes easily. Remove catfish and keep warm. Add
lemon juice to cream mixture. Reduce liquid to half over high
heat or until mixture is thick enough to coat a spoon. Spoon
sauce on serving plate and place catfish on sauce. Garnish with
parsley. Serve immediately.

Chinese Steamed Catfish

Serves 4

1 ½ pounds catfish fillets
1 teaspoon shredded ginger root
1 green onion, chopped fine
1 teaspoon fermented black beans
1 tablespoon soy sauce
1 tablespoon dry sherry
1 teaspoon red pepper flakes
1 tablespoon peanut oil

Place fish on oiled heatproof plate. Make sauce by combining
the remaining ingredients. Pour the sauce over fish in a Chinese
steamer. When the water boils, steam the fish 10 minutes for
every inch of thickness.

Stuffed Catfish

Serves 6

*6 5–7 ounce catfish fillets or 6 13–15 ounce
    whole catfish*
2 ½ cups stuffing mix
½ cup diced apples
½ cup crushed walnuts
½ cup raisins
⅓ cup evaporated milk
2 tablespoons brown sugar
1 large egg
6 lemon slices
½ cup French salad dressing
¼ pound butter (1 stick)
3 tablespoons lemon juice

Combine stuffing mix, diced apples, walnuts, raisins, milk,
brown sugar, and egg. Cook on low heat 10 minutes. Melt butter
in a saucepan, adding French dressing and lemon juice, simmer
for 15 minutes. Add ½ of butter sauce to stuffing and set other ½
aside for basting. Place stuffing in middle of fillets, roll up and
secure with toothpicks, or stuff into cavities of whole catfish.
Place on baking sheet and bake at 350 degrees for 15 minutes.
Remove and baste with remaining butter sauce.

Mexican Catfish Roulades

Serves 6

6 catfish fillets
1 teaspoon onion salt
3 ounces cream cheese, softened
2 tablespoons bottled onion salad dressing
3 ½ teaspoons taco seasoning mix
2 tablespoons chopped onion
2 tablespoons chopped celery
20 Ritz crackers, crushed
2 tablespoons melted butter
Fresh parsley to garnish
Lemon to garnish (optional)

Sprinkle fish with onion salt and set aside. Blend cream cheese, salad dressing, and 1 ½ teaspoons taco seasoning. Stir in onion and celery. Divide the mixture into 6 equal portions and place in middle of fillets; roll up the fillets and secure with toothpicks. Combine cracker crumbs and 2 teaspoons taco seasoning. Dip each fish roll in melted butter and roll in crumb mixture, coating well. Place rolls in greased baking dish and bake at 350 degrees for 30 minutes or until fish is browned and flakes easily.

Catfish Bienville

Serves 6–8

2 pounds catfish fillets
1 tablespoon melted butter
1 tablespoon lemon juice
1 teaspoon salt
⅛ teaspoon white pepper
Bienville sauce (below)
Parsley sprigs to garnish
Cherry tomatoes (optional)

Place fillets on well-greased rack of broiler pan. Combine butter, lemon juice, salt and pepper. Brush fillets with butter mixture. Broil 6 inches from heat for 8 minutes or until fish flakes easily. Remove fillets to warm serving platter. Spoon Bienville sauce over fish and garnish with parsley and cherry tomatoes.

Bienville Sauce

Makes about 3 cups

3 slices bacon, chopped
2 tablespoons butter
⅓ cup chopped green onions
¼ cup all-purpose flour

2 cups milk
½ pound processed cheese spread, cut into
small pieces
¼ cup sherry
4-ounce can sliced mushrooms, drained
½ pound cooked shrimp, chopped
¼ teaspoon Worcestershire
¼ teaspoon white pepper
Dash hot pepper sauce

Cook bacon and onion in medium skillet until bacon is light brown. Add butter and flour; simmer, stirring until smooth. Do not brown flour. Gradually add milk to make a smooth paste. Cook over low heat until thickened and bubbly. Add cheese and cook until melted. Stir in remaining ingredients.

Smoked Catfish

Rub 1 to 1½ pounds of whole catfish heavily with salt inside and out. Let stand overnight. Rub salt off catfish (or rinse and dry thoroughly afterwards), hand dry or lay catfish in open air for 1 hour to dry.

Lay or hang dried catfish in smoker so that the catfish are over a concentrated source of heat and smoke. Catfish should not be closer than 1 foot to the fire and heat must be evenly maintained throughout the smoking, which should take 9 to 12 hours.

When done, the catfish should be a rich saffron yellow color. Allow the catfish to cool on the grill for an hour or two before removing.

Onion-Baked Farm-Raised Catfish

Serves 6

2 pounds catfish fillets
1 cup sour cream
1 cup mayonnaise
1 package (4/10 ounce) ranch-style dressing mix
2 3-ounce cans fried onion rings

Combine sour cream, mayonnaise, and salad dressing mix in a medium-size bowl. Measure out ¾ cup of mixture and pour into a flat dish. Reserve remaining mixture to serve as sauce. Finely crush the onion rings and place in another flat dish. Dip fillets in salad dressing mixture and then roll in crushed onion rings. Place fish on an ungreased baking tray and bake at 350 degrees for 20 to 25 minutes, or until fish flakes easily. Garnish as desired and serve with the remaining salad dressing mixture.

Smoky Grilled Catfish Marinade

Serves 6

12 catfish steaks
⅓ cup soy sauce
3 tablespoons vegetable oil
1 tablespoon liquid smoke
1 clove garlic, chopped fine
½ teaspoon ginger
½ teaspoon salt
Lemon wedges

Combine all ingredients but catfish and lemons; mix well. Place fish in marinade for 30 minutes. Reserve marinade for basting. Grill catfish 3 inches from heat for 5 to 7 minutes. Turn and brush with marinade. Cook until fish is browned and flakes easily. Serve with lemon.

Zippy Grilled Catfish Marinade

Serves 6

12 catfish steaks
2 teaspoons salt
¼ teaspoon pepper
4 tablespoons lemon juice
1 ⅓ cups Italian salad dressing

Combine all ingredients but catfish and mix well. Marinate fish in sauce for 30 minutes. Reserve marinade for basting. Grill catfish 3 inches from heat for 5 to 7 minutes. Turn and baste with reserved marinade. Cook until fish is browned and flakes easily.

Catfish Hawaiian

Serves 8

2 pounds catfish fillets
1 cup flour
1 tablespoon salt
1 ½ cups cooking oil
1 13 ½-ounce can pineapple chunks
½ teaspoon dry mustard
¼ cup brown sugar
1 teaspoon salt
1 teaspoon cornstarch
¼ cup vinegar
1 tablespoon margarine
½ cup green pepper strips

Combine flour and 1 tablespoon salt. Dredge fish in mixture and fry fish in cooking oil for 4 to 5 minutes on each side, turning carefully. Drain on absorbant paper. Keep warm on serving platter.

Combine mustard, brown sugar, 1 teaspoon salt, and cornstarch in saucepan. Add vinegar and blend well. Stir in pineapple with juice. Cook over low heat, stirring constantly until sauce is thick and smooth. Add margarine and green pepper and cook for 2 to 3 minutes. Serve over fish.

Grilled Catfish with Salsa

Serves 4

> 4 4–5 ounce catfish fillets
> ½ teaspoon salt
> ¼ teaspoon white pepper
> Olive oil marinade
> Salsa

Sprinkle fillets with salt and pepper. Place fillets on well-greased grill and brush with olive oil marinade. Grill 10 minutes per inch of thickness, turning once, until fish flakes easily. Serve with salsa.

Olive Oil Marinade

Makes 2 cups

> ½ cup orange juice
> ½ cup red wine vinegar
> 1 teaspoon grated orange rind
> ½ teaspoon dried oregano leaves

½ *teaspoon salt*
¼ *teaspoon celery salt*
Pinch cayenne pepper
½ *cup olive oil*

In a medium bowl, combine all ingredients except olive oil and mix until smooth. Slowly whisk in olive oil. Refrigerate at least 1 hour.

Salsa

Makes 2 cups

2 *large ripe tomatoes, peeled, seeded, and*
 quartered
1 *clove garlic, peeled*
3 *scallions, chopped*
4 *ounces canned green chiles, chopped*
1 *teaspoon olive oil*
1 *tablespoon lime juice*
Salt and pepper to taste
Cilantro or parsley to taste

Combine tomatoes, garlic, scallions, and chiles in food processor or blender until coarsely chopped. Stir in olive oil and lime juice. Add salt, pepper, and cilantro or parsley to taste. Let stand one hour before serving.

Catfish and Sprout Pita Sandwich

Serves 6 to 8

¾ pound catfish fillets
¼ cup sherry
¼ cup white wine
1 teaspoon ground cumin
1 teaspoon Worcestershire sauce
Salt and pepper to taste
2 tablespoons cooking oil
½ red pepper, thinly sliced
¼ cup water
½ pound bean sprouts
2 jalapeno peppers, thinly sliced
6 scallions, in 1 ½-inch pieces
1 teaspoon minced ginger root
1 ½ teaspoon red wine vinegar
6 to 8 4-inch whole wheat pita breads

Cut catfish into strips. Mix together in bowl the sherry, white wine, cumin, Worcestershire, salt and pepper. Add catfish to marinate 15 minutes. Drain catfish and reserve marinade. Heat 1 tablespoon of oil in a 10-inch skillet. Cook fish for one brief minute, turning strips with a spatula. Lift out fish and set aside.

Pour the remaining oil into the skillet and add red pepper, cover and cook over medium heat for about 2 minutes. Meanwhile wash the sprouts and rinse under very hot water; drain well. Add the jalapeno peppers, scallions, ginger and sprouts to the skillet. Season with salt and pepper to taste. Stir to mix well, cover and cook for 30 seconds. Add vinegar and water to marinade. Pour mixture over contents in the pan. Cover and cook 1 minute. Return catfish to pan and remove from heat. Let stand for 30 seconds.

Toast the pita breads, slit to make pockets and spoon in about ½ cup of the mixture to fill each one.

Catfish Crepes

½ cup cornmeal
½ cup unbleached flour
1 ¼ cups water
2 eggs

Mix ingredients and using crepe pan prepare 8 crepes.

Catfish Crepes Filling

Serves 4

1 pound catfish, boiled and flaked
2 tablespoons oil
1 onion, minced
2 tablespoons whole wheat flour

2 cups skim milk
1 cup grated Parmesan cheese
½ cup grated mozzarella cheese
½ teaspoon salt
Grated Parmesan and parsley to garnish

Brown onions in oil. Add flour and mix until onions are coated. Add milk slowly; cook and stir until thickened. Add cheeses, salt, and fish. Cook until cheese melts. Roll mixture into crepes and close. Place in greased baking dish and cook at 350 degrees until heated through, about 10 to 15 minutes. Before serving sprinkle with Parmesan cheese and garnish with parsley.

Catfish Quiche

Serves 6

1 ½ pounds catfish, boiled and flaked
1 2-ounce can mushroom stems and pieces,
*   drained and chopped*
1 defrosted 9-inch unbaked pastry shell
¼ teaspoon liquid smoke
1 ½ cups shredded Swiss cheese
1 tablespoon instant minced onion
3 eggs

1 10¾-ounce can cream of onion soup
¾ teaspoon lemon pepper
⅛ teaspoon paprika
Parsley sprigs to garnish

Sprinkle 1 cup cheese over bottom of pastry shell. Using mixer, beat eggs and soup together in a bowl. Stir in flaked catfish, mushrooms, liquid smoke, minced onion, and lemon pepper. Pour mixture into pastry shell. Sprinkle with remaining ½ cup cheese and paprika. Place on baking sheet on lowest shelf and bake at 375 degrees for 35 to 40 minutes until golden brown and filling is set. Cool 10 minutes before serving. Garnish with parsley.

Baked Dixieland Catfish

Serves 6

6 whole catfish
½ cup bottled French dressing
12 thin lemon slices
Paprika

Brush catfish inside and out with French dressing. Cut 6 of the lemon slices in half, placing 2 halves in each fish. Place catfish on well-greased baking dish, and place a lemon slice on each. Brush top of the fish with remaining dressing and sprinkle with paprika. Bake at 350 degrees for 30 to 35 minutes until fish flakes easily with a fork.

Smoked Almond Catfish

Serves 4

4 4–5 *ounce catfish fillets*
¼ *cup liquid smoke*
1 ½ *cups water*
½ *cup packaged hushpuppy mix*
½ *cup chopped almonds*
2 *tablespoons melted butter*
Paprika
Salt and pepper to taste

Combine liquid smoke and water. Marinate fillets at least 15 minutes, making sure fillets are well covered. Drain. Combine hushpuppy mix and almonds. Baste fillets with butter and sprinkle with salt and pepper. Roll fillets in hushpuppy/almond mixture. Place on a rack in a baking pan. Sprinkle remaining hushpuppy/almond mixture over fillets and lightly sprinkle with paprika. Bake at 350 degrees for 35 minutes.

Stuffed Smoked Catfish

Serves 4

4 4–5 ounce catfish fillets
¼ cup liquid smoke
1 ½ cups water
1 ¼ cups corn bread stuffing mix
¼ cup hot water
2 ¼ tablespoons melted butter
Salt, pepper and paprika to taste

Combine liquid smoke and water. Marinate fillets at least 15 minutes, being sure that fillets are well covered. Drain, reserving marinade for basting. Combine stuffing mix with hot water and butter. Place ¼ of stuffing mix into each fillet. Roll-up and fasten with toothpicks. Baste with marinade. Sprinkle with salt, pepper, and paprika. Bake uncovered at 350 degrees for 25–30 minutes.

Catfish Eldorado

Serves 6

6 4–5 ounce catfish fillets
2–3 tablespoons bacon drippings
1 medium onion, diced
1 large clove garlic, diced

1 green bell pepper, diced
28 ounce can tomatoes
Tabasco sauce to taste
1 tablespoon Worcestershire
⅓ to ½ cup beer
½ teaspoon basil
1 bay leaf
½ teaspoon salt
⅛ teaspoon pepper
3 eggs, separated
4 tablespoons white flour
2 4-ounce cans green chili strips, peeled and
*   seeded*
6 ounces Monterey Jack cheese, shredded coarsely

Saute onion, garlic and bell pepper in 1 to 2 tablespoons bacon
drippings until softened. Add tomatoes and simmer 5 minutes.
Add Tabasco, Worcestershire, beer, basil, bay leaf, salt and
pepper. Simmer, stirring occasionally for 10–15 minutes. Meanwhile, prepare catfish. Preheat oven to 350 degrees. Melt drippings in frying pan to lightly cover bottom. Beat egg whites
until fluffy, and then fold in beaten yolks. Wash catfish in cold
water, drain and dredge in flour. Dip each into egg mixture and
cover immediately. Place fish in moderately heated frying pan
and brown lightly on each side. Remove fish and place in non-
greased baking dish. Lay 3 ½ inch wide strips of green chili

lengthwise on each fish. Cover with tomato sauce mixture. Bake in oven about 20 to 25 minutes or until fish flakes easily. Sprinkle grated cheese over fish during last 5 minutes of baking to melt.

Catfish Kiev

Serves 6

> 2 *pounds catfish fillets, cut into strips*
> 1 *teaspoon onion salt*
> 3 *ounce package of cream cheese with chives*
> 2 *tablespoons butter*
> 1 *teaspoon lemon pepper*
> 4 *ounces mushroom pieces, drained*
> ½ *cup melted butter*
> 1 ⅓ *cups seasoned croutons crumbs*
> *Parsley sprigs to garnish*

Divide fillets into 12 strips about 6 by 2 inches. Press lightly to flatten; sprinkle with onion salt. In a medium bowl, combine cream cheese, 2 tablespoons of margarine and lemon pepper. Stir in mushrooms. Divide cheese into 12 portions and place a portion at the end of each fish and roll up. Dip rolls into melted margarine and roll in crumbs. Place rolls on well-greased baking dish and drizzle with remaining margarine. Bake, uncovered at 350 degrees for 25 to 30 minutes. Garnish with parsley.

Blackened Catfish

Serves 6

6 4–5 *ounce catfish fillets*
½ *pound unsalted butter, melted*
1 *tablespoon sweet paprika*
2 ½ *tsp. salt*
1 *teaspoon onion powder*
1 *teaspoon garlic*
1 *teaspoon coarse ground pepper*
¾ *teaspoon white pepper*
¾ *teaspoon black pepper*
½ *teaspoon dried thyme leaves*
½ *teaspoon dried oregano leaves*
Fresh lemon juice

Preheat heavy [black] skillet. Combine seasonings in small bowl. Dip fillets in melted butter and then sprinkle seasoning mixtures on both sides. Place in hot skillet. Add 1 tablespoon butter over top of fillets. Cook for 2 to 3 minutes on each side until charred. Serve with a squeeze of fresh lemon juice.

ACCOMPANIMENTS

Quick and Easy Hushpuppies

*1 cup self-rising cornmeal (or 1 cup meal, 2
    teaspoons baking powder, 1 teaspoon salt)*
1 cup self-rising flour
1 tablespoon sugar
1 cup milk
1 egg
1 medium onion, finely chopped
½ bell pepper, chopped (or 1 jalapeno, chopped)
Vegetable oil

Combine cornmeal, flour, sugar, egg, onion, bell pepper, and
milk. Drop by tablespoonful into hot oil, about 370 degrees,
until golden brown on all sides. Drain on paper towels.

Hushpuppies

Makes 30 hushpuppies

Vegetable oil
¼ cup sugar
2 teaspoons baking powder
1 teaspoon salt
¼ teaspoon pepper
½ teaspoon garlic salt
⅔ cup chopped onion
1 egg, beaten
1 ¼ cup milk
1 ½ cup yellow cornmeal
1 ½ cup flour

Heat oil to 375 degrees in deep fryer or deep skillet. Mix sugar, baking powder, salt, pepper, and garlic salt. In blender, mix onion, egg, and milk to a smooth, thick consistency. Whisk together the two mixtures and let sit about 5 minutes. (Bubbles should begin to form.) Mix cornmeal and flour together and then gradually add to the liquid mixture. Drop dough by spoonfuls into the hot oil, frying only a few at a time, until golden brown, about 4 to 5 minutes. Remove with a slotted spoon and drain well on paper towels.

Kathy Starr's Hushpuppies

Makes 20 to 24

2 ½ cups cornmeal mix
1 tablespoon vegetable oil
1 cup onions, chopped
½ cup bell peppers, chopped
1 ⅓ cups buttermilk
3 cups oil for frying

In a bowl, mix cornmeal, oil, chopped onion, and bell pepper.
Mix well with buttermilk until firm for rounding off to hushpuppies. Heat 3 cups of vegetable oil in a deep fryer, dropping
hushpuppies singly by the spoonful, and frying them until golden
brown.

Another Hushpuppy

Makes 20 to 30

1 ¾ cups self-rising cornmeal (or cornmeal, 3
*   teaspoons baking powder and 1 ¾ teaspoons salt)*
1 ¼ cups buttermilk
1 small onion, chopped
1 egg, beaten
1 teaspoon salt

Pinch of cayenne
Pinch of garlic powder
3 tablespoons bacon drippings
Oil for frying

Mix cornmeal, salt, sugar, cayenne and garlic powder. Mix together the buttermilk and egg and add gradually to the meal mixture. Slowly add onion and heated bacon drippings. Drop singly by the spoonful into hot oil, frying until they are golden brown.

Yet Another Hushpuppy

1 teaspoon baking soda
1 ½ cups buttermilk
1 ½ cups yellow cornmeal
½ cup all-purpose flour
Pinch salt
1 small onion, diced fine
Pinch black pepper
Oil for frying

Mix baking soda with buttermilk, and then mix with cornmeal and flour. Add salt, onion, and pepper, mixing well. Drop batter by spoonfuls into hot oil (375 degrees). Cook until browned.

Coleslaw

Serves 10 to 15

4 to 5 pounds cabbage, shredded
2–3 large sweet onions, chopped
1 ½ cups peanut oil
1 cup vinegar
1 tablespoon Dijon mustard
½ cup sugar

Toss together the cabbage and onions in large bowl. Place the oil, vinegar, mustard, and sugar in a saucepan and bring to a boil. Pour over cabbage and mix. Chill, stirring occasionally.

Kathy Starr's Slaw

Serves 8 to 10

1 large head green cabbage, shredded
½ cup purple cabbage, shredded
½ cup onions, finely chopped
1 cup sweet pickle relish
¼ cup sugar
1 cup salad dressing
1 small carrot, grated
⅛ teaspoon salt

In a large bowl, combine all ingredients. Mix thoroughly and chill.

Yogurt Coleslaw

1 head of green cabbage, shredded
1 ⅓ cup yogurt
3 tablespoons vinegar
2 tablespoons sugar
1 teaspoon salt
1 small onion, chopped

Toss together cabbage and onion. Then add other ingredients, stirring well. Chill 1 hour or longer until serving.

Fried Dill Pickles

1 cup very cold water
1 cup self-rising flour
1 egg
Dill pickles, chilled
Vegetable oil for frying

Mix water, flour, and egg. Drain dill pickles and dip in batter. Set in refrigerator to chill, while oil gets hot (375 degrees) in a deep fryer or deep skillet. Place pickles singly in oil, and fry a few at a time, until golden. Drain on paper towels. Serve hot.

Craig Claiborne's Baked Grits

Serves 6 to 8

1 cup regular or quick-cooking grits
½ pound grated sharp cheddar cheese
8 tablespoons butter
3 eggs, well beaten
⅓ cup plus 1 tablespoon milk

Preheat oven to 350 degrees. Cook the grits according to package directions. Stir in the cheese, butter, eggs, and milk, and pour into a buttered 3-cup baking dish. Bake 40 minutes or longer, until set.

Baked Garlic-Cheese Grits

Serves 4 to 6

1 cup quick-cooking grits
6 ounces garlic cheese (or 1 ½ cups cheddar and 1
*   teaspoon chopped garlic)*
8 tablespoons butter

½ *chopped scallions, including green part,*
   optional
2 *eggs, lightly beaten*
¾ *cup milk*

Cook the grits according to the package directions. Stir in the
cheese, butter, and scallions. Pour the mixture into a buttered
2-quart casserole. Let cool. Preheat the oven to 375 degrees.
Blend the eggs and milk and pour over the grits. Bake about
1 hour.

French Fries—Variations

For a variation on the everyday french fries, try dredging them in
cornmeal before frying, salted and peppered to taste. Or use
sweet potatoes or a mixture of sweet and Idaho potatoes.

BIBLIOGRAPHY

Altman, Chris. "Tips & Tricks for Spawning Catfish," *Southern Outdoors,* April 1990, pp. 33–39.

Alva, Marilyn. "Chi-Chi's Franchise Group to Women: Let's Have Lunch," *Nation's Restaurant News,* October 27, 1986, p. 14.

Axelrod, Herbert R.; Emmens, Cliff W.; Sculthorpe, Duncan; Vorderwinkler, William; Pronek, Neal; and Burgess, Warren E. *Exotic Tropical Fishes.* Neptune, N.J.: T.F.H. Publications, 1981.

Bardach, J. E.; Todd, J. H.; and Crickmer, R. "Orientation by Taste in Fish of the Genus Ictalurus," *Science,* March 18, 1967, pp. 1276–1278.

Bashline, Sylvia. *Cleaning & Cooking Fish.* Minnetonka, Minn.: Publication Arts, 1982.

Blassingame, John W. *The Slave Community: Plantation Life in the Antebellum South.* New York: Oxford University Press, 1979.

Botkin, B. A. *A Treasury of American Folklore: Stories, Ballads, and Traditions of the People.* New York: Crown Publishers, 1944.

Botkin, B. A. *A Treasury of Southern Folklore: Stories, Ballads, Traditions and Folkways of the People of the South.* New York: Crown Publishers, 1953.

Bourne, Wade. "Reservoir Catfish," *Southern Outdoors,* June 1990, pp. 51–53.

Brewer, John Mason. *American Negro Folklore.* Chicago: Quadrangle Books, 1968.

BIBLIOGRAPHY

"Carnivorous Catfish Something Less Than Duck's Delight," *Houston Post,* 22
 April 1989, p. A25.

Cassidy, Frederick, ed. *Dictionary of American Regional English.* Cambridge: Belknap
 Press of Harvard University Press, 1985.

Catfish Farmers of America. *The Catfish Journal.* Jackson, Mississippi.

Catfish Farmers of America. Recipe cards. Jackson, Mississippi.

Catfish Institute. *Fishing for Compliments: Cooking with Catfish.* Belzoni, Mississippi,
 1987.

"Catfish raised on a farm, in a controlled environment are a healthful choice,"
 Detroit Free Press, 21 September 1990, p. 3B.

Cederberg, Goran, ed. *The Complete Book of Sportfishing.* New York: Bonanza Books,
 1988.

Cerame, Jon. *From Greasy Row to Catfish Capital.* Oxford, Miss.: Rebel Press, 1978.

Circle, Homer, and Lycock, George. "America's Six Most Popular Sport Fish,"
 Boy's Life, April 1985, p. 31+.

Claiborne, Craig. *Craig Claiborne's Southern Cooking.* New York: Times Books, 1987.

Cook, Fannye A. *Freshwater Fishes in Mississippi.* Jackson, Miss.: Mississippi Game
 and Fish Commission, 1959.

Dalrymple, Byron W. "The Catfish Boom," *Field & Stream,* March 1990, pp.
 102–107.

Dalrymple, Byron W. "The Catfish Connection," *Field & Stream,* July 1987,
 p. 72+.

Dalrymple, Byron W. *Sportsman's Guide to Game Fish.* New York: World Publishing
 Co., 1968.

DeSilva, Cara. "Catfish Swimming in New Waters," *Newsday* (Long Island, New
 York) 28 February 1990. Section—Food, p. 4.

Douglas, Ellen. *White Cloud, Black Cloud.* Jackson: University of Mississippi Press,
 1989.

Dunbar, Tony. *Delta Time: a Journey Through Mississippi.* New York: Pantheon
 Books, 1990.

Eddy, Samuel. *How to Know the Freshwater Fishes.* William C. Brown Publishers,
 1969.

Embry, Mike. "Kentucky Strives to Make a Splash in the Catfish Market," *Lexington Herald Leader* (Kentucky), 3 September 1989, p. D1.

Fabricant, Florence. "Catfish Head Out of the South to Claim Nationwide Popularity," *Nation's Restaurant News* 28 August 1989, p. 11.

Farr, Sidney Saylor. *More than Moonshine: Appalachian Recipes and Recollections.* Pittsburgh: University of Pittsburgh Press, 1983.

Fast, Barry (ed.) *The Catfish Cookbook.* Charlotte, N.C.: East Woods Press, 1982.

Fritz, Michael. "Catfish, Cajun Style, in Moscow," *Forbes Magazine,* 12 December 1988, pp. 37–38.

Gershwin, George. *Porgy and Bess.*

Grzimek, Bernhard, ed. *Grzimek's Animal Life Encyclopedia,* v. IV. New York: Van Nostrand Reinhold, 1973.

Hayward, Du Bose. *Porgy.* New York: Grosset and Dunlap, 1925.

Hilliard, Sam Bowers. *Hog Meat and Hoecake: Food Supply in the Old South, 1840–1860.* Carbondale: Southern Illinois University Press, 1972.

Holland, Gina. "Mississippi Catfish Gaining Nation's Notice," *Vicksburg Evening Post* (Mississippi). 22 January 1990, p. A3.

"It's Catfish to Go, Shrimp to Come: Aquaculture's Growing on U.S.," *Quick Frozen Foods International,* October 1989, p. 68+.

Jefferson, Thomas. "Notes on the State of Virginia," in *Writings.* New York: Library of America, 1984.

"John Folse, Lafitte's Landing Restaurant Presents Sauteed Filet of Catfish, Sauce Meunier," *Restaurant Business Magazine,* 10 August 1986, p. 233+.

Koller, Larry. *The Treasury of Angling.* New York: Golden Press, 1963.

Larsen, Larry. "Monster Cats of Texas," *Outdoor Life,* July 1985, pp. 88–89.

Lewis, Jack. "Cats Can Be Easy," *Outdoor Life,* June 1983, p. 74+.

Livingston, A. D. "Tight Lines at Taylor's," *Field & Stream,* April 1990, pp. 20–22.

MacCormack, Zack. "Catfishing in Williamson County," *Austin American-Statesman* (Texas), 7 June 1990, section—Neighbor, p. 1+.

Madson, John. "To Catch This Fish, Put Hand in Mouth, Hang On—and Pull," *Smithsonian Magazine,* September 1984, p. 54+.

Maleskey, Gale. "Catfish Slime: a Natural Cure for Cuts?" *Prevention,* June 1988, p. 12+.

BIBLIOGRAPHY

Maloy, Charles R. and Willoughby, Harvey. *Rearing Marketable Channel Catfish in Ponds.* Washington: Bureau of Sport Fisheries and Wildlife, Resource Publication 31, January 1967.

McGee, William Mitchell; Dellenbarger, Lynn E.; and Dillard, James G. *Demographic and Attitudinal Characteristics of Catfish Consumers.* Mississippi State: Mississippi Agricultural and Forestry Experiment Station, Technical Bulletin 168, December, 1989.

McWhirter, Norris and McWhirter, Ross. *Guinness Book of World Records, 1986.* New York: Sterling Publishing Company, 1985.

Meyers, Chet and Linder, Al. *Catching Fish.* Minneapolis: Dillon Press, 1978.

Morris, Willie. *North Toward Home.* Oxford, Miss.: Yoknapatawpha Press, 1967.

Murphey, Fred. "It's Time to Plant Trees, Shrubs, Fish," *Akron Beacon Journal* (Ohio), 25, March 1988, p. B2.

Nelms, W. C. "Reservoir Catfish Raising," *Mississippi Game and Fish,* October, 1964, p. 7.

Parsons, P. Allen. *Complete Book of Fresh Water Fishing.* New York: Outdoor Life, 1963.

Peck, Ted. "How to Find and Catch More Channel Cats," *Fishing Facts,* August 1990, pp. 45–48.

Perrin, Gail. "Catfish Out of the Bag: a Farm-Bred Delicacy," *Akron Beacon Journal* (Ohio), 2 October, 1988, p. A3.

Peterson, David. ". . . As Big as a Man?" *Mother Earth News,* June 1988, pp. 53–57.

Pote, Jonathan; Wax, Charles L.; and Tucker, Craig S. *Water in Catfish Production: Sources, Uses, and Conservation.* Mississippi State: Mississippi Agricultural and Forestry Experiment Station, Bulletin 88-3, November 1988.

"Record Catfish Turns Out Fishy, But Remains Flat-Out Whopper," *Detroit Free Press,* 21 September 1990, p. 38.

Reed, Julia. "A Fish Tale Worth Telling," *U.S. News & World Report,* 10 November 1986, p. 66.

Rice, F. Phillip. *America's Favorite Fishing.* New York: Harper & Row, 1964.

Robertson, James. *Dycus v. Sillers.* 557 Southern Reporter 2d. 486 (Miss. 1990).

Sanfield, Steve. *The Adventures of High John the Conqueror.* New York: Orchard Books, 1989.

Seay, James. *Let Not Your Hart.* Middletown, Conn.: Wesleyan University Press, 1970.

Selman, Frank B. "Grabbin' Cats," *Outdoor Life,* March 1983, p. 84+.

Singleton, Theresa A. (ed.). *The Archaeology of Slavery and Plantation Life.* Orlando: Academic Press, 1985.

Smith, Frank. *The Yazoo River.* New York: Rinehart, 1954.

Stern, Jane and Stern, Michael. "A Taste of America," *Newsday* (New York), 17 August 1988, section—Food, p. 5.

Stevens, Rose Budd. *Along the RFD with Rose Budd Stevens.* Jackson: University Press of Mississippi, 1987.

Swanton, John R. *The Indians of the Southeastern United States.* Washington: Smithsonian Institution Press, 1979.

Swingle, H. S. "Commercial Production of Red Cats (Speckled Bullheads) in Ponds," *Southern Fisheries Society Meeting.* Little Rock, Arkansas: October 1956. (Mimeographed)

Taylor, Joe Gray. *Negro Slavery in Louisiana.* Baton Rouge: Louisiana Historical Association, 1963.

Twain, Mark. *The Adventures of Huckleberry Finn.* Pleasantville, N.Y.: Readers Digest Association, 1986.

Twain, Mark. *Life on the Mississippi.* Pleasantville, N.Y.: Readers Digest Association, 1987.

Twain, Mark. *Mississippi Writings.* New York: Literary Classics of America, 1982.

"Verastility," *New Yorker,* 28 May 1990, pp. 30–31.

Volkart, Bill. "Fine Lines to Fat Cats," *Field & Stream,* July 1990, p. 42+.

Walton, Izaak and Cotton, Charles. *The Compleat Angler: or the Contemplative Man's Recreation.* New York: A. L. Burt Co., n.d.

Weintz, Mark. "Bag of Tricks for Cats," *Southern Outdoors,* June 1990, p. 10.

"We Salute the Industry of Mississippi Farm-Raised Catfish," *Yazoo Herald* (Mississippi), 1 April 1987, supplement, section D.

Williams, C. Herb. "Fat Cats of the Northwest," *Outdoor Life,* June 1983, p. 74+.

BIBLIOGRAPHY

Williams, Mina. "Value-added Catfish Lures New Customers," *Supermarket News,*
    4 June 1990, p. 32+.
Wilson, Charles Regan and Ferris, William (ed.). *Encyclopedia of Southern Culture,*
    Chapel Hill: University of North Carolina Press, 1989.
Wise Encyclopedia of Cookery. New York: Grosset & Dunlap, 1971.
"World Catfish Special Issue," *People's Press,* (Yazoo City, Miss.). 4 April 1987,
    pp. A1–A48.
Wulff, Lee (ed.). *The Sportsman's Companion,* New York: Harper & Row, 1968.
Zuckerman, Dave. "Catfish Gains in Popularity: 1985 Sales Could Reach 185
    Million Pounds," *Nation's Restaurant News,* 28 October 1985, p. 1+.

INDEX

INDEX